THE
Chafing Dish
Cookbook

H. W. DOREMUS

THE

Chafing Dish

Cookbook

by

John and Marie
Roberson

illustrated by
H. W. Doremus

PRENTICE-HALL, INC.   NEW YORK

Second printing, December, 1950
Third printing, February, 1951
Fourth printing, April, 1951
Fifth printing, August, 1951
Sixth printing, July, 1952
Seventh printing, December, 1952
Eighth printing, April, 1953

PRINTED IN THE UNITED STATES OF AMERICA

Without the congenial collaboration of these two friends, this volume might never have reached the printer's hands:

GERTRUDE BLAIR,

friend of long standing. One of the best-known food consultants in America, Gertrude has worked with high imagination for leading packaged food companies and advertising agencies. Her skill has proved invaluable in the advising, checking, and kitchen-testing of recipes in *The Chafing Dish Cookbook*.

STAN. JONES,

writer, traveler, gourmet, friend. Stan. Jones has known the fine foods and rare wines of France on many occasions, is an excellent amateur chef currently specializing in chafing dish cookery.

Salut!

Contents

CONTENTS

CONTENTS

[ix]

CONTENTS

CONTENTS

CONTENTS

THE
Chafing Dish
Cookbook

THINGS YOU'LL NEED
TO KNOW

The chafing dish is a symbol of some of the best things our civilization has produced—good fellowship, good living, good conversation, and, above all, good food. As such, it has a history and a character all its own. Many of us, the authors included, have come to know the chafing dish the hard way, through trial and error. In the hope of sparing you the error and making the chafing dish your instant and constant friend, we have summed up our experience in this book.

Triumphal Return

For almost ten years, we have alternately bored and delighted friends with that most versatile adjunct of gourmet cooking, the chafing dish. We have probably bored them with its praises. We have sent them into gurgling ecstasies over the miracles whipped up in its gleaming pan. In our streamlined, servantless apartment, this darling of world-famous chefs has held sway over old friends, youngsters about town, and even men and women who enjoyed after-theater snacks in the glorious gaslight era. It has proved a faithful friend and companion under every kind of social stress.

The triumphal return of the chafing dish to a place of honor in these utilitarian days has been a surprise to many, but there are solid reasons for its reappearance on the scene. Despite its aura of glamour, it is an intensely practical utensil. It is handsome, versatile, portable, quick and easy to use. It glorifies both the cook and his cooking.

City folk, cramped in boxlike apartments, are exploring with glad cries the manifold uses of the chafing dish. More hosts and hostesses than ever are making the happy discovery that applause can follow their ministrations with chef's apron and spoon—and applause is meat and drink to the ego.

Romance and a certain elusive enchantment surround the supper for two when the male (or female) touch is in evidence amid the glow of shining metal. Soft music provides the obbligato, subdued lighting lends its charm. Under such circumstances, with the foodstuffs cunningly arranged in the foreground and a bottle nestling in its gleaming bucket, only enchanted evenings can result!

Enthusiastic amateur chefs who awe their guests with a single spectacle such as *Pêches Flambées Eau de Vie de Framboise* may not know how exceedingly versatile the chafing dish can be. Some of these manifold uses will be explored in the pages of this cookbook.

Unlike your bulky though utilitarian stove, the chafing dish —a gracious addition to the table in itself—can play many roles. It is extremely mobile. It may be carried into the living room, out on the terrace, or down to the rumpus room. On the buffet, your chafing dish is invaluable for keeping canapés and hors d'oeuvres warm.

People who entertain at home know the chafing dish as a friend indeed—one which can double in brass. Whether one decides upon a steaming potage ladled from a *Petite Marmite*, a noble *Chafing Dish Breast of Chicken in Sherry Sauce*, or a blazing dessert such as *Cherries Jubilee*, your copper cook may be employed. (And *this* cook makes no demands for raises, for rest, or for the evening off!)

Above all, the chafing dish is a gift from heaven to the man or woman who admits to a flair for cooking. For here is an instrument superbly designed to give full scope to the showmanship latent in most human beings! You arise, your audience seated expectantly before you. Under their intent and wondering eyes a savory meal is whipped up—presto! No interruption in the conversation. No running out to the kitchen. No awkward pauses while waiting for something to cook on top of a stove. Here, right on your own stage, your dish is prepared deftly, graciously, with all the airs of a continental chef.

It is true that most of us associate the chafing dish with the turn of the century, when it played an important role in casual entertaining. (We used to listen, with a certain nostalgia, to tales of the delicate, creamy concoctions kept warm on family buffets till the ladies should arise from the whist tables to the accompaniment of a genteel creaking of high-boned corsets.) This, however, was no more than the modern version of a very ancient and historic cooking utensil. Its use goes back, some historians surmise, even to biblical times. It is an established fact that chafing dishes were found in the ruins of Pompeii— and Pompeians lived very well indeed. The chafing dish gets its name, by the way, from the Latin word *calefacere*, to make warm, and its Middle English derivative *chaufen*, which has the same meaning. At one time it was called a "cheffing dish."

In Victorian England, in France, and in the early days of this republic, the chafing dish was a prized family possession. Virginia gentlemen bequeathed them to their offspring and to favored nephews and nieces. In 1711, a Mr. Thomas Chisman left two beautiful brass chafing dishes and one iron one to his heirs and assigns. The relicts of Lieutenant Governor Fauquier, and those of a Lord Botetourt, presumably squabbled over possession of the superbly designed English chafing dishes which had belonged to the deceased.

No doubt the modern chafing dish is vastly different from

its ancestor of olden times, but its purpose remains the same: to cook food easily and in an attractive manner. Today's version is light and portable, easily stowed away in a closet when not in use. It is most frequently created in gleaming copper, with blazer and hot water pan lined with block tin. Planned by artists who skillfully blend utility with gracious design, today's chafing dish is enjoying an extraordinary re-birth of popularity.

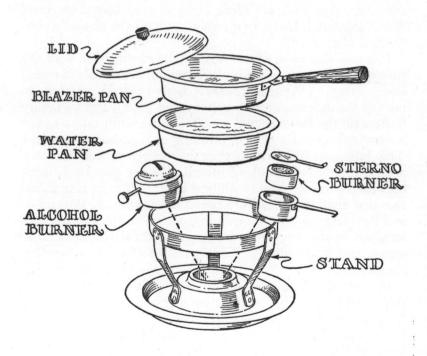

LID

BLAZER PAN

WATER PAN

STERNO BURNER

ALCOHOL BURNER

STAND

The Chafing Dish Family

There are several different types of chafing dishes in general use today. They are made differently for different purposes, though *all* chafing dishes serve as a means of gracious and portable entertaining.

DOUBLE BOILER

1. The most popular type is the two-quart size chafing dish. It is made of copper, block-tin lined, and includes a water pan. This pan is the original of our American double boiler; in the modern chafing dish, it performs a very important function, controlling the heat transference to the food pan and thereby regulating the smoothness of the food. Furthermore, it permits careful mixing without discoloration or lumpiness.

This "double boiler" chafing dish is suitable for cooking such dishes as *Lobster Newburg* and *Welsh Rabbit*. It is ideal for keeping foods warm at the table, and for keeping hors d'oeuvres and sauces at an even temperature without danger of burning them.

2. Another style of chafing dish is what might be called the "skillet type." This is an inexpensive set which consists of a single pan and cover used for cooking over a direct hot flame, just as a skillet is used over a regular stove.

Quick dishes, such as bacon, ham, flaming shrimp, chicken livers, and certain kinds of sauces, thrive on this kind of chafing dish.

SINGLE PAN

3. A third type of chafing dish, popular for many generations in European homes, clubs, hotels, and on steamship lines, might be characterized as a "warmer." This dish is on the large side and is used exclusively to keep food warm; it is heated only by an alcohol wick.

WARMING DISH

4. The shallow crêpes suzette pan is the fourth member of the family. Used in hotels and smart French restaurants, it is made of copper, lined with silver, and measures about twelve inches in diameter. On this highly specialized type of chafing dish the little pancakes are at their best, cooked in the presence of the diners. Just before serving a flaming brandy is poured over them, creating a scene dear to the heart of the exhibitionist.

5. The *petite marmite*, or earthenware casserole, is a type of chafing dish frequently used over a low flame for soups and slow-cooked "one-dish meals." Actually the *petite marmite* belies its name, since it is a large, deep pot which holds from four to six quarts. It is extremely useful for large gatherings—especially for those *unexpected* large gatherings.

Smaller earthenware casseroles are sometimes used over an asbestos pad on alcohol or Sterno burners.

6. A newcomer to the family of chafing dishes has just been placed on the market. It is an electric chafing dish which, like other electric appliances, may be plugged into any outlet. It has two ranges of heat, high and low, with an automatic thermostat control. Since it cannot be used beyond the range of an outlet, it will have limited portability. Then, too, the glamour of the true chafing dish flame will be somewhat dimmed. Nevertheless, an electric chafing dish has distinct possibilities.

From experience we have found that the most satisfactory unit for all-purpose use is the alcohol-burner chafing dish with a blazer and water pan. It combines all the advantages of a portable stove and gives a strong heat which can be easily and quickly regulated from an intensely high heat to a modest warming flame. This is the favorite of the professional maître d's and experienced amateur chefs who prefer the ultimate in efficient equipment.

THINGS YOU'LL NEED TO KNOW

Which Heating Unit Will You Use?

Four types of heating apparatus are commonly used in chafing-dish cookery.

1. The first of these employs alcohol for fuel. Because it is designed to intensify heat, the burner reaches a high temperature in a very short time. On the other hand, this highly versatile burner may be adjusted to a slow, lazy flame if you so desire. As to cost, alcohol is considerably cheaper than Sterno. It may be purchased very reasonably by the quart or gallon, and will last somewhat longer than solid fuel.

2. Another type employs the solidified alcohol known as "Sterno." Being a lazy flame, it is especially well adapted to slow cooking or keeping foods warm. If given ample time, however, "canned heat" can be used for almost any purpose. Because it is sold in small tins at a relatively high price, Sterno is fairly expensive if used consistently in your chafing dish.

3. A third type of heating unit is the wick alcohol burner, which is similar in principle to the old kerosene lantern. Its flame is relatively small and provides little heat. For this reason it is best adapted to chafing dishes used solely as food warmers. This particular type of burner goes back to the old days in England, when sumptuous feasts were the rule. At such mighty table jousts, these chafing dishes (then called "warming pans") played an important part in keeping the multiple courses warm on the sideboard until serving time.

4. Electric chafing dishes should come with complete instructions. They are easy to use; however, the heat control is slower to regulate, and in some instances it is wise to remove the blazer from the heat until the coils have changed temperature. This is probably the least expensive unit to operate.

Heat Control for Fuel Burners

Quick changes of cooking heat are vitally important to chafing dish cookery. Heat may be regulated by any of the following methods:

1. Opening the aperture wide to allow maximum heat, then sliding the cover over the opening to reduce the heat to the desired intensity. In some instances, the cap of the Sterno can may be employed as the cover or heat control.

2. Using the water pan, filled with hot water, in much the same manner as a double boiler. We have already explained how this arrangement serves to control heat and assure the smoothness of the food.

3. Using asbestos pads to lower heat and prevent staining of copper utensils.

Petite Marmite

Electric

How to Care for Your Chafing Dish

First, let us congratulate you on being the proud possessor of a chafing dish! We envy the many exciting discoveries in gourmet cooking which lie before you. Nor will you ever regret buying this book. A small investment in itself, it will repay you in new and delicious dishes—and in the gracious mode of entertaining which the chafing dish makes possible.

Copper Is Quicker!

Let us assume that the chafing dish you have purchased is made of copper and lined with block tin. Copper is the most popular metal for the "red metal" is one of the finest conductors of heat known to man, and with a block-tin lining it is ideal for cooking and serving gourmet dishes. Foods cook more uniformly in copper; heat penetrates the metal so easily that an even cooking of the entire dish is assured.

THINGS YOU'LL NEED TO KNOW

Before Using

Before going into action with your new chafing dish, we suggest that you run scalding water inside the cover and the food pan. *After* use, wash the copper surfaces in hot running water, using a brush with soap to remove food particles. Then rinse in warm water and dry with a soft towel.

In the event of discoloration of the copper exterior, an extra-fine steel wool soap pad is excellent, always providing that your hand movement in cleaning slowly follows the contour of the article. Jerky, short motions must be avoided. There are now countless fine copper polishes on the market.

The Block-Tin Surface

Never use coarse abrasives on your tin linings, or on any processed or plated wear. And never use metal spoons or forks in your chafing dish. *Always* use wooden forks and spoons.

We suggest that you wash the tin lining of your chafing dish in the usual manner. Of course, when you wash the pan as just directed, the *inside* has to be washed, too.

If desired, Bon Ami powder is good for additional care. A final word of caution: please don't expect to secure quite the same blinding rosy finish which distinguished your chafing dish when brand new. It simply can't be done.

Tray-Maid

Your tray becomes your maid in chafing dish cookery. Be sure that she gives good service. Most confirmed chafing dishers have found that a large oblong tray is a necessity; the oblong shape seems to lend itself to a greater variety of arrangements than any other style.

You'll save yourself a lot of trouble if you check the contents of your tray-maid against the recipe each time you plan to use your chafing dish. Be sure you include any extras your own original version of the recipe may require. Numbers have been provided in the Tray-Maid section for your convenience in checking items on your tray behind the scenes.

Neatness of arrangement and neatness of preparation of the materials themselves (precise slicing, shredding, etc.) aids immeasurably in creating eye appeal. It takes only a few seconds more to prepare food artistically, but it pays off very handsomely indeed. Careful arrangement often provides striking color contrasts.

Here is a list of standard Tray-Maid accessories:

> Variety of small dishes
> Pepper and salt grinders
> Wooden spoons
> Sauce and condiment containers
> Small wire whisk
> Measuring spoons
> Cruets for oil, vinegar, wine
> Asbestos pad

Six General Ideas

1. In chafing dish cookery it is better to roll patties, croquettes, and the like in bread or cracker crumbs rather than flour. This gives them a firm, crisp outside crust.

2. Kitchen Bouquet adds a clever touch to your chafing dish meats. If brushed on the meat before cooking, it imparts a rich brown color to the finished product. Any of the following extracts will produce the same effect: Gravy Secret, Maggis, Gravy Brown, Meat Glaze, or any other agent used in strengthening and coloring soups and gravies.

3. Make use of the water pan of your chafing dish to keep hot dishes hot for serving.

4. Since your audience seldom misses a trick, appearance counts double in chafing dish cookery! Here are a few suggestions for keeping up appearances all through the cooking and serving periods:

   a) *Never* appear with all the ingredients in a heap on the Tray-Maid and then toss them into the chafing dish at one fell swoop. Instead, arrange them in a pattern with eye

We Suggest . . . Some Pantry Foods for Easy Chafing Dish Use

Breads

biscuits, several kinds
cocktail snacks
tiny rolls
toast

Soups

keep a full stock of your
    favorites

Fish and Seafood

anchovies, plain, rolled,
    stuffed
anchovy paste
barbecued crab legs
clams, minced or whole
crabmeat, varied forms
finnan haddie
frogs' legs à la Newburg
green turtle meat
herring fillets and kipper paste

lobster meat and paste
oyster stew and gumbo
sardines
shad roe
shrimp in varied forms
snails
tuna fish

Meats and Poultry

bologna and other smoked
    sausage
Brunswick stew
chicken
chicken giblets
corned beef, plain and hash
dried beef
frankfurters
goose liver pâté
ham à la king
ham, devilled and boiled
liver

pheasant à la Newburg
pork and beans
roast beef in cans
Spam
tongue
turkey, smoked
Virginia ham paste

Desserts

babas au rhum
bar le duc
black cherries
crêpes suzette
fig pudding
fruits in syrup or brandy, all
    kinds
fruits macedoine
kumquats
marrons
orange slices
plum pudding

Dessert Sauces

brandied hard sauce
brandied peach sauce
melba sauce

Miscellaneous

antipasto
artichoke hearts
cheese of all kinds
chutney
hollandaise sauce
mushrooms
nuts of all kinds, plain and
    salted
olives, green, ripe, stuffed
onion, pearl, raw
potatoes julienne
Welsh rabbit

And . . .

frozen foods of all kinds

appeal and add them to the chafing dish one at a time.
b) Cut the ingredients into neat uniform shapes. In some cases, old-fashioned cookie cutters can be used to advantage.

c) For a main dish which is creamed, or for one which emphasizes the sauce, be sure to reserve a little of the main ingredient, cut into decorative form. Add this at the end of the cooking period or just after cooking is completed.

d) When added to a mixture, sour cream looks most appetizing in the beginning. However, it soon begins to dry out and crack if simply spread over the top of the dish. This can be avoided by keeping a reserve supply of sour cream on hand and lacing the surface of the dish with it at the end of the cooking period. It should then be served at once.

5. Garlic can be used in several ways, but you should always take care that no whole particles remain in the dish at serving time. Try the following methods of using garlic in your favorite dishes:

a) Spear it on a toothpick, to be fished out when dish is finished

b) Mince and mash it to a paste with salt, using the flat of a knife

c) Mince and mash it without salt

d) Crush in the new garlic press.

6. Browned flour is a pleasant addition to many chafing dish recipes, particularly those in which wine and spices are used. To brown, spread the flour out in a shallow pan and place in quick oven (375°F.). Stir from time to time until all flour is browned. To brown on top of stove, put flour in heavy frying pan and stir until all flour is browned. Store in covered jar. Use as needed.

NOW you've got your chafing dish.

NOW you know how to use it and care for it.

NOW all we can do is wish you:

Bon appetit!

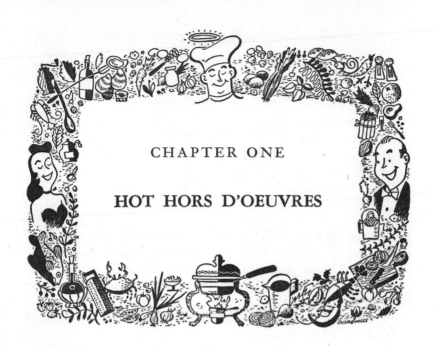

CHAPTER ONE

HOT HORS D'OEUVRES

Hot hors d'oeuvres are always tastier than their frigid brothers. The small toil involved in readying these small heavenly bodies will be repaid a thousand times by observing the warmth of their reception. Your eyes will witness one of the world's great unspoken compliments! P.S.: Be sure to keep a fine supply of paper napkins handy.

Shawl Rolls

bread   fillings
butter   chili powder

Behind the Scenes — Prepare fillings (recipes below). Remove crusts from very thin slices of bread. Spread each slice with butter and then with fillings. Roll the squares picking up one corner and rolling toward center. This will make a slender roll of bread with a shawl point on one tip. Pin with toothpick. Press a little flat. Wrap in moist (not wet) cloth.

Before the Guests — Melt a little butter in the blazer pan of chafing dish. Add a shake of chili powder. When piping hot, remove toothpick and toast the shawl rolls in this until brown on both sides. Repeat until all are brown. Serve on toothpicks.
Note: For extra flavor, rub the blazer pan with cut surface of a half clove of garlic.

Roquefort

1 package cream cheese (3 ounces)
1 portion Roquefort (½ ounce)
¼ teaspoon Worcestershire sauce
cream

Crabmeat

1⅓ cups crabmeat, flaked
2 teaspoons minced green pepper
2 teaspoons Worcestershire
2 teaspoons chili sauce

Liver

1 cup mashed cooked liver
2 tablespoons minced cooked bacon
4 drops Tabasco
1 teaspoon lemon juice

Tray-Maid

1) shawl rolls
2) butter
3) chili powder
4) garlic, if desired

[18]

Dunking Barbecue Sauce

¼ cup butter, margarine or oil
1 clove garlic, mashed to pulp
1 large onion, minced fine
1 teaspoon sugar
1 teaspoon salt
1 teaspoon dry mustard
1 teaspoon paprika
1 to 2 teaspoons chili powder
½ teaspoon pepper
1 tablespoon Worcestershire
   sauce
2 tablespoons lemon juice
1 tablespoon fresh herbs,
   minced
2½ cups tomatoes

Behind the Scenes — Prepare cooked seafood, fowl or meat for dunking by cutting into cubes. Mash garlic and mince onion. Mince fresh herbs (dry may be used if fresh are not obtainable)—basil, parsley, mint, thyme, sweet marjoram.

Before the Guests — Measure all ingredients for sauce into blazer pan and simmer until blended. Keep hot over hot water.

Tray-Maid	*Dunking*
1) meat, cooked and cubed	oysters
2) seafood, cooked and cubed	shrimp
3) fowl, cooked and cubed	cooked tongue, cubed
4) butter	snappy cheese
5) garlic and onion	cooked turkey or chicken
6) spices and seasonings	
7) lemon	
8) herbs	
9) tomatoes	

Dunking Sauce Supreme

1 cup (8 ounces) currant jelly
⅔ cup prepared mustard
2 medium-sized onions, grated

Behind the Scenes — Cube the meats neatly for dunking. Grate the onion.

Before the Guests — Stir jelly, prepared mustard and onion in blazer pan over flame until jelly is softened. Beat well. Place over hot water and the sauce is ready for guests to dunk.

Tray-Maid	*Dunking*
1) meats for dunking	boiled ham
2) jelly	delicatessen sausage such as
3) prepared mustard	bologna
4) grated onion	Spam
	Prem, etc.

Brownies

codfish balls	fine dry crumbs
chili balls	butter
pâté balls	seasonings
cream cheese balls	lemon juice
snappy cheese balls	watercress

Behind the Scenes — Select the balls you wish to serve (recipes below). Mix ingredients of each in order named. Shape into small balls and roll in the fine crumbs.

Before the Guests — Melt butter in blazer pan. Add seasonings to your taste (a bit of mustard or caraway seed, an herb such as thyme or orégano). Heat the balls in this until browned all over. Add a squeeze of lemon juice and a sprig of parsley or watercress and impale on a toothpick.

Codfish Balls

1 cup cooked codfish, shredded
1 cup fluffy mashed potatoes
   seasonings
   crumbs

Chili Balls

1 pound ground beef
1 onion, finely minced
1 teaspoon chili powder
   salt, pepper to taste

Pâté Balls

1 cup liver pâté

Cream Cheese Balls

3 ounce package cream cheese
⅛ pound bleu cheese

Snappy Cheese Balls

½ pound soft snappy cheese

Tray-Maid

1) brownie balls ready for blazer
     pan
2) butter
3) your choice of seasonings
4) cut lemon
5) watercress

Toast Quickies

bread
spreads
butter
seasonings

Behind the Scenes — Cut sliced bread, white, whole-wheat and rye, into small fancy shapes with cookie cutters. Select spreads for recipes below and mix.

Before the Guests — (Note: Bits of toast that have grown cold before serving are tough and tasteless—get out your chafing dish and toast as served.) Heat small amount of butter in blazer pan with half clove garlic. Discard garlic. Fry toast as needed. Let guests spread their own.

Savory Variations

Cream butter in portion with any one of the following:
chili sauce; finely minced mint; Indian chutney; ground smoked ham; well-mashed, skinless, boneless sardines; well-mashed shrimps.

Avocado Butter

½ cup butter
1 large ripe avocado
   juice of 1 lemon
Beat together pear pulp and butter. Thin and smooth by adding lemon juice a little at a time.

Lobster Butter

½ cup butter
½ cup lobster
   powdered mustard to taste
Warm butter slightly. Mash the lobster to a paste with the butter. Warm this paste. Mash through a sieve over a bowl of cold water. Skim off the butter when all has risen to top of water.

Anchovy Butter

½ cup butter
½ cup anchovy paste
   pinch of grated nutmeg
3 dashes paprika
1 teaspoon grated Parmesan
   cheese
Work together with a wooden spoon.

Tray-Maid

1) bread cut into fancy shapes
2) butter
3) seasonings of your choice
4) garlic
5) spreads

[22]

Pâté Crumpets

liver pâté
bread
butter
celery julienne
caraway seeds

Behind the Scenes — Slice bread very thin. Remove crusts. Spread with butter, sprinkle lightly with caraway seeds. Spread with liver pâté. Roll up each slice (like a cigarette) enclosing a long sliver of celery julienne in each. Fasten with toothpick. Wrap in moist (not wet) cloth (in groups of 8 or 10) and chill for 2 or 3 hours.

Before the Guests — Melt butter in blazer pan and a sprinkle of caraway seeds. In this toast the crumpets. Serve piping hot on toothpicks.

Tray-Maid

1) rolled crumpets
2) butter
3) caraway seeds

Special Filling

1 dozen chicken livers broiled
2 sweet pickles
½ cup celery leaves
    chili sauce
    dash Tabasco
Broil the livers. Then put through meat grinder several times, the livers, pickles and celery leaves. Add chili sauce to make a paste that will spread. Add Tabasco. Will make ⅓ cup of spread.

Triple-Play Chicken Cartwheels

chicken paprika wheels
chicken pineapple wheels
chicken almond wheels

½ cup butter
dry mustard
dash salt
bread

Behind the Scenes — Prepare the three fillings (recipes below).   Take a loaf of bread and remove all crusts; then cut thin slices the *length of the loaf*.   Spread with butter, then with filling.   Roll each slice like a jelly roll and fasten with toothpick.   Wrap in damp (not wet) cloth and refrigerate several hours.   Just before guests arrive, remove from wrappings and cut the rolls into slices ¼ inch thick.
Note: Select a variety of breads if your party is a big one. Use white bread for one filling; whole wheat for another; rye for a third.

Before the Guests — Melt enough butter in blazer pan of chafing dish to grease bottom of pan.   Add just a touch of the seasonings.   Toast the cartwheels in this and serve on toothpicks.

Paprika

1 cup minced cooked chicken
⅛ cup cream
3 tablespoons sweet pickle relish
   paprika

Pineapple

¾ cup cooked chicken
⅛ cup crushed pineapple drained
3 tablespoons mayonnaise

Almond

1 cup finely chopped cooked chicken and giblets
½ cup chopped toasted almonds
1 tablespoon onion
½ teaspoon curry
¼ cup mayonnaise

Tray-Maid

1) cartwheels
2) butter
3) seasonings

[24]

Bacon Wrap-Ups

oysters in bacon
pickles in bacon
chicken livers in bacon

stuffed olives in bacon
juice of 1 or 2 limes or lemons
minced parsley

Behind the Scenes — Wrap oysters, pickles, chicken livers and olives as directed in recipes below. Mince about ½ cup parsley.

Before the Guests — Get blazer pan piping hot. Broil the roll-ups as needed. Squeeze a little lemon juice over each before serving and add a sprinkle of parsley. Serve on toothpicks.

Oysters in Bacon

1 pint oysters, drained
1 pimiento, cut in strips
⅛ teaspoon garlic salt
2 tablespoons parsley, minced
  bacon

Season oysters with garlic salt; roll in parsley. Place strip of pimiento on each and wrap in bacon. Secure with toothpick.

Stuffed Olives in Bacon

large olive, stuffed
chicken pâté, ham spread or liver
  sausage
bacon

Remove pimiento stuffing from olives. Stuff with either chicken pâté, ham spread or liver sausage. Roll in bacon. Secure with toothpick.

Chicken Livers in Bacon

10 chicken livers
¼ teaspoon garlic salt
  paprika
  bacon

Cut livers in halves. Parboil 2 minutes. Season with garlic salt; dust with paprika. Roll in bacon. Secure with toothpick.

Masked Pickles

tiny sweet gherkins
cocktail onions
bacon

Drain gherkins and onions. Place one of each in a slice of bacon and wrap. Secure with toothpicks.

Tray-Maid

1) roll-ups ready for pan-broiling
2) lemon or lime cut in half
3) minced parsley

[25]

egg stars
ham crescents
crabmeat moons
sweet butter

4 tablespoons hickory-smoked
   salt
1 tablespoon paprika
   dash cayenne
⅛ teaspoon thyme

Behind the Scenes — Prepare the stars, crescents and moons. Mix the hickory-smoked salt, paprika, cayenne and thyme. Blend well and fill a small salt shaker.

Before the Guests — Melt butter in blazer pan of chafing dish and toast the tiny sandwiches as needed. Sprinkle with your own specially prepared seasoning. Serve on toothpicks.

Egg Stars

4 hard-cooked egg yolks, sieved
1 teaspoon prepared mustard
¼ teaspoon Worcestershire sauce
⅛ teaspoon salt
⅛ teaspoon pepper
1 teaspoon catsup
1 teaspoon grated onion
Cut bread into star shapes.
Spread mixture on star, top with a second.

Ham Crescents

1 cup minced boiled ham
¼ teaspoon ground cloves
¼ teaspoon mace
⅛ teaspoon salt
4 tablespoons cream
Cut bread into crescent shapes. Spread mixture on one crescent, top with another.

Crabmeat Moons

1 cup flaked crabmeat
1 tablespoon capers
   mayonnaise to bind
Cut rounds of bread. Spread on round with mixture, top with another round.

Tray-Maid

1) toasties ready for blazer pan
2) butter
3) special salt

[26]

Hi-Hat Mushrooms in Wine Sauce

16 medium-sized mushrooms
½ pound sausage meat
1 cup tomato sauce (6- or 8-
     ounce can)
1 cup white wine
½ clove garlic, mashed to pulp
⅛ teaspoon orégano

Behind the Scenes — Wash mushrooms. Remove and chop stems. Add these to sausage meat. Stuff the caps, rounding the sausage meat into a high crown. *Place in moderate oven (350°F.) and cook for one half hour (sausage meat must always be thoroughly cooked).* For the sauce, mince the garlic and then mash to a pulp to have ready for the sauce.

Before the Guests — Heat in blazer pan, the tomato sauce, wine, garlic and orégano. When blended add the hi-hat mushrooms. Cover and let sauce bubble over top. Spear with toothpicks for guests to nibble.

Tray-Maid

1) prepared hi-hats
2) tomato sauce
3) wine
4) garlic, mashed to pulp
5) herbs

Anchovy Meat Balls

 1 pound ground beef
 2 teaspoons minced olives
 ⅛ teaspoon brown sugar
 2 onions, finely minced
 2 slices bread, soaked in water
     and pressed out
   dash of Tabasco
   stuffed, rolled anchovies
   crumbs
 6 tablespoons butter
   oil from anchovies
 1 clove garlic
 1 teaspoon lemon juice
 1 ripe tomato, skinned, cut fine
 2 tablespoons red wine

Behind the Scenes — Make up the meat balls, mixing together the beef, minced olives, brown sugar, onions, moist bread and Tabasco. Roll into small balls (about 1½ inches in diameter). Press a caper-stuffed, rolled anchovy onto the top of each. Roll in crumbs.

Before the Guests — Melt butter in blazer pan of chafing dish and brown all the meat balls. Transfer to another dish. To the drippings in the blazer pan add remaining ingredients and simmer to a rich sauce. Discard garlic. Reheat anchovy meat balls and keep hot over hot water or low flame for constant serving.

Tray-Maid

 1) anchovy meat balls
 2) butter
 3) anchovy oil
 4) garlic on toothpick
 5) lemon for juice
 6) tomato cut fine
 7) wine

Cheese Tidbits au Beurre Noir

    butter or bacon drippings
  2 to 3 drops Kitchen Bouquet
  ⅛ teaspoon onion or garlic salt
    lemon juice, if desired
    cheese balls
    rice balls

Behind the Scenes — Prepare the cheese balls and the cheese and rice balls.

Before the Guests — Melt butter or bacon drippings in blazer pan. Add Kitchen Bouquet and onion or garlic salt. Drop in the cheese or cheese and rice balls and toast until golden brown and cooked through. Squeeze on lemon juice and serve.

Cheese Balls

  ⅓ teaspoon salt
  ⅛ teaspoon mustard
    pinch cayenne
1½ cups grated cheese
  3 egg whites, beaten stiff
  1 tablespoon minced parsley
  ½ cup bread crumbs
Mix all ingredients except crumbs and blend. Form into small balls the size of a marble. Roll in bread crumbs.

Cheese and Rice Balls

  1 cup cooked rice
  1 egg
  1 tablespoon milk
  ½ cup grated cheese
  2 teaspoons mustard
  ¼ teaspoon salt
  ¼ teaspoon paprika
  ½ cup bread crumbs
Mix all ingredients except crumbs together. Shape into small balls. Roll in bread crumbs.

Tray-Maid

  1) butter
  2) Kitchen Bouquet
  3) onion or garlic salt
  4) prepared cheese tidbits
  5) lemon juice

To Stuff . . . Sautéed Mushrooms

2 pounds mushrooms with:
Chili Cheese Stuffing
Chicken and Almond
Tasty Salmon
Egg and Lobster

Behind the Scenes — Carefully wash and stem good-sized mushrooms. Prepare fillings for stuffing.

Before the Guests — Melt butter in blazer pan of chafing dish. Sauté whole mushrooms until slightly browned. Remove to a platter and let the guests help themselves and do their own selection of stuffing.

Chili Cheese

⅓ cup chili sauce
½ cup grated cheese
¼ cup cottage cheese
1 teaspoon prepared mustard

Chicken and Almond

1½ cups minced cooked chicken
½ cup blanched chopped almonds
½ pepper (green) minced
⅓ teaspoon salt
⅛ teaspoon paprika
pinch of grated lemon rind
½ cup mayonnaise

Tasty Salmon

1 cup canned salmon
1 teaspoon capers
1 tablespoon chopped gherkins
1 tablespoon minced green olives
1 tablespoon minced parsley
1 teaspoon lemon juice
mayonnaise to bind

Egg and Lobster

1 cup lobster, minced
4 hard-cooked eggs, riced
1 cup hot curry sauce
Combine and keep warm over hot water.

Tray-Maid

1) mushrooms, prepared
2) prepared stuffings
3) butter for sautéeing

3 tablespoons butter
3 tablespoons flour
¾ cup chicken stock
¾ cup cream
½ onion
¼ pound grated Parmesan cheese
¼ pound Swiss cheese
For dunking
1) cooked shrimp
2) cubed ham
3) cooked tongue sticks
4) cubes of whole-wheat or
rye bread toasted

Behind the Scenes — Prepare your shrimp, fresh or from can. Cut boiled ham (or delicatessen smoked sausages) into cubes. Cut tongue into strips. Toast cubes of rye and whole wheat bread.

Before the Guests — Melt butter in blazer pan of chafing dish. Blend in flour. Add onion, chicken stock and cream, gradually. Cook, stirring until sauce thickens. Remove onion. Place over hot water, add cheese, and cook gently over low flame until well blended.

Tray-Maid

1) cubes for dunking of shrimp,
etc.
2) butter
3) flour
4) chicken broth (canned may
be used)
5) onion
6) cheese
7) cream

Be Your Own Author

And *this* space is yours alone . . . reserved for your notes, personal recipes, and favorite clippings . . . use it!

CHAPTER TWO

COME FOR SOUP AND SALAD

Well-organized executives will extol the seeming simplicity of this type of menu. They will think: "Ah, if I were a bachelor, this is precisely what *I'd* do!" Their wives, well aware of the pre-battle handiwork, will extol them, too. They'll also phone next morning for your recipes.

Chicken Soup Supreme

10½-ounce can cream of chicken
    soup
10½-ounce can chicken soup with
    rice
water
¼ cup cream
⅛ teaspoon curry powder
¼ cup California Rhine Wine
    (sauterne or any white
    wine)
watercress to garnish

Behind the Scenes — Open tins of chicken soup and pour directly into blazer pan of chafing dish. Add equal amount of water. Mix curry powder smoothly with the cream and add to soup. Place in refrigerator until needed.

Before the Guests — Stir soup directly over the flame until it begins to thicken, then continue stirring carefully until piping hot or place over water pan for safety's sake and heat more slowly until hot. Add wine. Garnish and serve at once. Serves 4.

Tray-Maid	*Menu*
1) mixed soups, cream and curry powder mixed	Shrimp Cocktail
2) wine	Chicken Soup Supreme
3) garnish	Green Goddess Salad
	Poppy Seed Rolls
	Grapes and Pears with Cheese
	Coffee

Sherry Mongole

1 can condensed tomato soup
1 can condensed green pea soup
¾ cup water
1 cup light cream
2 teaspoons Worcestershire
sauce
5 tablespoons sherry

Behind the Scenes — Open tins of soup and combine with water in blazer pan of chafing dish. Measure cream. Prepare salad greens and keep crisp in refrigerator.

Before the Guests — Heat soup over low flame, stirring until smooth. Add cream; stir in Worcestershire. Heat thoroughly. Remove from flame and add sherry slowly. Serve immediately. Serves 4 to 6.

Tray-Maid	*Menu*
1) cream	Sherry Mongole
2) Worcestershire	Western Salad Bowl
3) sherry	Blueberry Muffins
4) measuring spoon	Coffee
	Liqueur

Hearty Corn Chowder

2 tablespoons butter or marga-
    rine
2 tablespoons flour
1 large onion, sliced
2 cups diced potatoes
1½ cups whole kernel corn
    (canned)
1 teaspoon salt
⅛ teaspoon pepper
½ teaspoon curry powder
1 quart milk
paprika

Behind the Scenes — Cook potatoes in jackets, pare and dice. Slice onion. Remove corn from tin. Measure butter and flour.

Before the Guests — Melt butter in blazer pan of chafing dish. Add onion and sauté until soft and golden; do not brown. Blend in flour. Add milk gradually. Keep flame low. Add corn and stir until mixture thickens slightly. Add potatoes and seasoning. Heat until piping hot. Serve with a sprinkling of paprika. Serves 4 to 6.

Tray-Maid	*Menu*
1) butter	Hearty Corn Chowder
2) potatoes, cooked and diced	Tomato and Cottage Cheese Salad
3) measured butter on waxed pa- per	Crusty Rolls
4) flour	Fresh Fruit Cup
5) curry powder	Coffee
6) onion, sliced	
7) corn	
8) milk	
9) paprika, pepper, salt	

Quick Vegetable Soup with Meat Garnish

        ½ pound ground beef
        1 teaspoon salt
        ⅛ teaspoon pepper
        ¼ teaspoon allspice
        2 tablespoons onion, minced
        1 small clove garlic, minced
        2 10½-ounce cans condensed
            vegetable soup
        milk
        2 tablespoons butter or marga-
            rine
        2 tablespoons parsley, minced

Behind the Scenes — Combine ground beef, salt, pepper, all-spice, onion and garlic.   Remove soup from tins and thin with milk to desired consistency.   Mince parsley.

Before the Guests — Melt butter or margarine in blazer pan of chafing dish. Drop the meat mixture by teaspoonfuls and brown lightly on all sides.   Stir in soup and heat gently to piping hot.   Add parsley.   Serves 4 to 6.

Tray-Maid

1) butter
2) meat, prepared
3) soup combined with milk
4) parsley, minced

Menu

Quick Vegetable Soup
with Meat Garnish
Corn Sticks
Tomato-Cucumber Salad
Date and Nut Loaf with
Whipped Cream
Coffee

Boston Clam Chowder

2 dozen shucked clams with
liquor
¼ pound salt pork, cubed
2 medium-sized onions, sliced
2 cups diced cooked potatoes
1 teaspoon salt
¼ teaspoon pepper
1 quart milk
1 tablespoon flour

Behind the Scenes — Cook potatoes in jackets, cool, pare and dice. Drain clams thoroughly, reserving clam liquor. Pass clams through fingers and remove any bits of shell. Cut the soft part of the clams away from the hard part. Chop the hard portion finely and keep the soft portion whole. Cube salt pork and cook it in chafing dish, saving both pork and drippings. Slice onions.

Before the Guests — Heat salt pork drippings in blazer pan. Add onions and cook until soft and tender; stir occasionally; do not brown. Blend in flour. Add seasonings. Stir in milk and cook until slightly thickened. Add chopped clams and cook slowly for 5 minutes. Add clam liquor, potatoes and soft part of clams. Heat gently for 10 minutes. Just before serving add the crisp salt pork bits. Serve with split biscuit on top. Serves 4 to 6.

Tray-Maid

1) potatoes, cooked, pared and
   diced
2) clams separated; soft part
   whole, hard part chopped
3) crisp salt pork
4) onion, sliced
5) clam liquor
6) flour
7) milk
8) Pilot Biscuits
9) salt and pepper

Menu

Boston Clam Chowder
Pilot Biscuits
Vegetable Salad Bowl
Gingerbread
Coffee

Crab Bisque

3 tablespoons butter or margarine
3 tablespoons flour
1 teaspoon salt
⅛ teaspoon pepper
3 cups milk
1 cup chicken bouillon or chicken broth (homemade or canned)
1⅓ cup crab meat (6½-ounce tin)
1 onion, sliced
⅛ teaspoon powdered mace or nutmeg
2 tablespoons parsley, minced
½ cup light cream or top milk

Behind the Scenes — Remove crab meat from tin. Flake and run fingers through to remove bits of cartilage. Slice onion. Mince parsley.

Before the Guests — Melt butter or margarine in blazer pan of chafing dish. Blend in flour. Season with salt and pepper. Add milk gradually with the chicken bouillon. Stir over low heat until rich and creamy thick. Add crab meat, onion, parsley and mace or nutmeg. Cover; simmer 10 minutes. Add cream and cook another 5 minutes. Garnish with parsley and serve hot. Serves 4 to 6.

Tray-Maid	*Menu*
1) butter or margarine	Crab Bisque
2) flour	Tomato-Avocado Salad
3) salt and pepper	Cheese Sticks
4) milk	French Pastry
5) chicken bouillon	Coffee
6) crab meat, flaked	
7) onion, sliced	
8) parsley, minced	
9) mace or nutmeg	
10) cream	

Jiffy Chicken-Cucumber Soup

10½-ounce can condensed
　　chicken soup
½ cup milk
1 cup light cream
2 eggs, slightly beaten
½ teaspoon salt
2 cucumbers
⅛ teaspoon freshly ground pep-
　　per
⅛ teaspoon paprika

Behind the Scenes — Pare cucumbers and cook in small amount of salt water. Mash and measure to make 1 cup purée.

Before the Guests — Combine soup, milk, salt, pepper and cream in blazer pan of chafing dish, place pan over flame and heat to boiling. Add cucumber purée. Beat eggs in mixing bowl; pour hot soup over eggs and stir to blend. Return to blazer pan and heat thoroughly but do not boil. Sprinkle each serving with paprika. Serves 4.

Tray-Maid	*Menu*
1) soup combined with milk	Jiffy Chicken-Cucumber Soup
2) salt, pepper	Molded Asparagus Salad
3) cream	Hot French Bread
4) cucumber purée	Minted Melon Ball Cup
5) eggs	Coffee
6) paprika	

One-Two-Three Minestrone

2 cups consommé (canned or
  homemade)
½ cup cooked cabbage
½ cup corn (canned) optional
½ cup cooked lima beans (fresh,
  frozen or canned)
½ cup cooked onions
1 cup cooked tomatoes
1 cup water
1 teaspoon salt
¼ cup cooked macaroni
  Parmesan cheese, grated

Behind the Scenes — Have all vegetables cooked and ready for use. Be sure to cut the vegetables into neat strips before cooking.

Before the Guests — Place all ingredients except cheese in blazer pan of chafing dish. Cook for 15 minutes. Serve piping hot with grated cheese over top. Serves 4 to 6.

Tray-Maid	*Menu*
1) consommé	One-Two-Three Minestrone
2) all vegetables, cooked	Italian Bread Sticks
3) water	Caesar Salad
4) salt	Pears with Bel Paese Cheese
5) macaroni, cooked	Coffee
6) cheese, grated	

Consommé with Avocado

5 cups beef consommé
2 tomatoes, skinned, sliced
½ cup dry sherry
¼ cup American Burgundy
1 teaspoon salt
¼ teaspoon freshly ground pepper
1 avocado, peeled and diced

Behind the Scenes — If canned consommé is used, dilute as directed on can, then measure for required 5 cups. Scald, skin and slice tomatoes. Peel and dice avocado.

Before the Guests — Place all ingredients except avocado in blazer pan. Heat soup, steaming hot. Garnish with diced avocado just before serving. Serves 4.

Tray-Maid

1) beef consommé
2) tomatoes, skinned and sliced
3) sherry
4) burgundy
5) salt, pepper
6) avocado, diced

Menu

Consommé with Avocado
Artichoke and Onion Salad
Toasted Rolls
Lemon Soufflé
Coffee

Onion Soup

½ cup butter or margarine
3 large onions, sliced
dash of Maggi seasoning
1 teaspoon salt
½ teaspoon freshly ground pepper
2 teaspoons flour
4 cups chicken stock
½ cup grated Parmesan cheese
2 cloves garlic, crushed
4 slices French bread

Behind the Scenes — Prepare French bread by cutting loaf diagonally in four pieces, cutting so that knife does not quite reach the bottom of loaf. Spread surface of each slice first with butter, then with crushed garlic. Heat in moderate oven (350° F.) 10 minutes just before serving. Slice onions.

Before the Guests — Melt butter in blazer pan of chafing dish. Add onions, salt, pepper. Cook over low heat until onions are golden brown (about 15 minutes), stirring frequently to prevent any burning. Blend in flour. Add chicken stock and Maggi seasoning, stirring constantly until it comes to a boil. Simmer gently 15 minutes. Pour into onion soup bowls. Float a piece of garlic bread in each bowl. Sprinkle with grated cheese. Serves 4.

Tray-Maid	*Menu*
1) butter	Onion Soup
2) flour	Garlic Bread
3) chicken stock	Tomato and Dill Salad
4) Maggi seasoning	Blackberry Shortcake
5) onions	Coffee
6) salt, pepper	
7) garlic French bread	
8) Parmesan cheese	

2 dozen oysters with liquor
1 quart rich milk
2 tablespoons butter
1 tablespoon parsley, minced
⅛ teaspoon celery salt
½ teaspoon salt
⅛ teaspoon pepper
⅛ teaspoon mace

Behind the Scenes — Strain oysters and reserve the liquor. Run fingers through oysters to remove bits of shell. Mince parsley.

Before the Guests — Place oysters, milk and liquor in blazer pan and heat gently until steaming hot and until oysters begin to curl at edges. Add butter, mace, seasonings and chopped parsley. Serve piping hot. Serves 6.

Tray-Maid	*Menu*
1) oysters with liquor	Oyster Stew
2) butter, measured out on waxed paper	Sea Biscuits
	Molded Cucumber Salad
3) milk	Macedoine of Fruit with
4) seasonings	Crest of Currant Jelly
5) chopped parsley	Coffee
6) mace	

Asparagus Soup

1 pound fresh or 1 package
    frozen asparagus
1 medium onion sliced
2 cups hot water
3 egg yolks
1½ teaspoon salt
¼ teaspoon freshly ground pep-
    per
    paprika
2 cups cold rich milk or half
    milk, half cream
    whipped cream (optional)

Behind the Scenes — If fresh asparagus is used wash and place it with onion and water in sauce pan. Cover and simmer gently until vegetables are quite soft. Put through strainer. Separate eggs and reserve whites for some future dish.

Before the Guests — Place asparagus and onion pulp in blazer pan of chafing dish with hot water. Add egg yolks, salt and pepper. Stir with wooden spoon over moderate heat until mixture begins to thicken. It must *not* boil. Add milk. Heat thoroughly over hot water and serve at once. Soup may be garnished with a spoonful of whipped cream topped with a sprinkle of paprika. Serves 4.

Tray-Maid	*Menu*
1) hot water	Asparagus Soup
2) asparagus and onion pulp	Cheese Sticks
3) egg yolks	Deviled Egg Salad
4) salt, pepper	Eclairs filled with Ice Cream
5) milk and cream	Coffee
6) whipped cream, if desired	
7) paprika	

Potato and Chive Soup

    5 small potatoes
    1 bunch scallions, minced
    1 medium onion, sliced
    1 cup water
    ½ tablespoon salt
    ¼ teaspoon freshly ground pep-
       per
    1 cup heavy cream
    1 cup rich milk
    ¼ cup chopped chives

Behind the Scenes — Peel and slice potatoes. Chop scallions. Peel and slice onion. Place in saucepan with the water, salt and pepper. Cover and cook until vegetables are mushy (about 40 minutes). Rub through a fine strainer. Chop chives.

Before the Guests — Place all ingredients except chives in blazer pan of chafing dish. Stir over low heat until well mixed and piping hot. Garnish with chives. Serves 4.

Tray-Maid	*Menu*
1) vegetable pulp	Potato and Chive Soup
2) cream	Pumpernickel Bread
3) milk	Crisp Vegetable Salad
4) chopped chives	Apricot Cobbler
	Coffee

Garlic Soup with Poached Eggs

2 cloves garlic
⅓ cup oil (preferably olive oil)
3 slices French bread, cubed
½ teaspoon paprika
1 quart beef, veal or chicken
   broth (homemade or canned)
salt and pepper
4 to 6 eggs (1 egg per person)

Behind the Scenes — Cube French bread. Mince garlic. Measure oil into blazer pan of chafing dish. Brown garlic in oil; add bread cubes and toss them in the oil. Remove bread cubes from pan. Add paprika and broth. Season to taste. Remove from heat until ready to start cooking for the guests.

Before the Guests — Place blazer pan over flame. Cook soup for 15 minutes. When almost ready to serve break into the broth as many eggs as desired and poach. Serve soup with an egg in each plate; garnish with bread cubes. Serves 4 to 6.

Tray-Maid	*Menu*
1) eggs	Avocado Salad
2) bread cubes	Garlic Soup with Poached Eggs
	Toasted French Bread
	Grapefruit Halves with
	Cherry Cordial poured into center
	Coffee

Bisque of Seafood

2 cups crabmeat, lobster meat or
    shrimp, cooked and cleaned
10½-ounce can cream of celery
    soup
3 cups milk
1 pint cream
1 stalk celery, very thinly sliced
½ teaspoon salt
2 dashes of Tabasco sauce
¼ teaspoon powdered mace
1 egg
3 tablespoons sherry

Behind the Scenes — Cut seafood into neat strips. Strip the celery of all strings and fiber; slice *very thin*. Mix celery soup, cream and milk.

Before the Guests — Turn soup mixture into blazer pan of chafing dish. Heat. Add celery, salt, Tabasco and powdered mace. Cover; simmer about 2 minutes to heat celery through. Stir in egg yolk and add seafood. Stir gently until steaming hot. Place over hot water. Add sherry. Reheat if necessary and serve at once. Makes 6 cups.

Tray-Maid	*Menu*
1) celery	Avocado with Watercress
2) soup, cream, milk mixture	French Dressing
3) seasonings	Bisque of Seafood
4) seafood	with Bread Sticks
5) egg yolk	Fruit Tart
6) sherry	Coffee

Corn Bisque

4 tablespoons butter
3 tablespoons flour
1 teaspoon salt
¼ teaspoon pepper
3 cups milk
1½ cups canned corn
1½ cups canned tomatoes
4 cloves (whole)
1 bay leaf

Behind the Scenes — Combine the tomatoes, cloves and bay leaf. Cook for 5 minutes. Strain.

Before the Guests — Melt butter in blazer pan. Blend in flour; add seasonings. Gradually add milk, stirring constantly until thickened. Add corn; cover and cook for 10 minutes. Add the strained tomatoes to the milk mixture, stirring constantly. Reheat to piping hot. Serve at once. Serves 6.

Tray-Maid	*Menu*
1) butter	Corn Bisque
2) flour	Chef's Salad
3) seasoning	Popovers
4) milk	Ice Cream Cake Roll
5) corn	Coffee
6) strained tomatoes	

Holiday Soup

- 4 tablespoons butter
- 4 tablespoons flour
- 1 teaspoon salt
- ⅛ teaspoon freshly ground pepper
- 4 cups milk
- 1 cup cooked squash (fresh or frozen)
- 6 roasted chestnuts, shelled
- ½ teaspoon dried orange peel
- ½ teaspoon onion juice
- ¼ teaspoon ginger
- ½ cup heavy cream
- ⅛ teaspoon nutmeg
- 1 teaspoon paprika

Behind the Scenes — Heat squash and chestnuts together with a little water. Drain; put through strainer and add grated orange peel. Whip cream with nutmeg.

Before the Guests — Melt butter in blazer pan of chafing dish. Blend in flour. Gradually add milk and stir constantly until mixture begins to thicken. Season with salt and pepper. Add the squash-chestnut mixture; then add onion juice and ginger. Cook slowly, stirring often for 10 minutes. Serve topped with whipped cream sprinkled with paprika. Serves 6.

Tray-Maid	*Menu*
1) butter	Holiday Soup
2) flour	Turkey Salad
3) milk	Crusty Rolls Cranberry Jelly
4) squash-chestnut	Apricot Parfait
5) onion juice	Coffee
6) ginger	
7) whipped cream	
8) paprika	

Delicate Clam Bisque

  1 can minced clams (10 ounce
      can)
  1 cup water
  ½ cup American dry wine (sau-
      terne, sherry, Rhine Wine)
  2 tablespoons butter
  ¼ teaspoon salt
  ⅛ teaspoon freshly ground black
      pepper
  ½ cup thin cream
  3 egg yolks
      chopped chives
      paprika

Behind the Scenes — Open tin of clams. Mince chives. Beat egg yolks into cream.

Before the Guests — Add water, wine, butter, salt and pepper to clams in blazer pan of chafing dish and simmer on low flame for 5 minutes. Add cream and egg yolk mixture; place over hot water and stir until mixture begins to coat the spoon and thickens. (Take care not to let mixture boil, as it will curdle.) Serve immediately in slightly heated dishes. Sprinkle with chives and paprika. Serves 4.

Tray-Maid	*Menu*
1) clams	Zucchini Salad
2) water	Delicate Clam Bisque
3) wine	Toasted Rolls
4) butter	Lemon Meringue Pie
5) cream and egg yolks	Coffee
6) salt, pepper	
7) chives, minced	
8) paprika	

Mushroom Bisque

1 pound button mushrooms
4 cups chicken broth
4 tablespoons butter
3 tablespoons flour
¼ teaspoon dry mustard
½ teaspoon salt
⅛ teaspoon freshly ground pepper
1 teaspoon paprika
¼ cup sherry
½ cup heavy cream

Behind the Scenes — Wash and remove stems from mushrooms. Chop stems finely and add to chicken broth with seasonings. Simmer 30 minutes; strain.

Before the Guests — Melt butter in blazer pan of chafing dish. Sauté the mushroom caps to a delicate brown. Sprinkle the flour over mushrooms, then dry mustard and stir until flour is blended with butter. Gradually add the chicken broth and continue stirring until mixture thickens. Place pan over hot water and cook for 10 minutes. Add more seasoning at this point if necessary. Stir in sherry and cream. Cook 2 minutes longer. Serve in individual bowls with paprika dusted on top. Serves 4.

Tray-Maid

1) mushroom caps
2) butter
3) flour
4) mustard
5) salt, pepper
6) paprika
7) chicken broth
8) sherry
9) cream

Menu

Mushroom Bisque
Toasted Cheese-Sprinkled
Crackers
Potato Salad
Melon Ball Fruit Cup
Coffee

Ham and Chicken Gumbo

2 tablespoons butter
¼ pound boiled ham, cut julienne
¼ cup green onions, minced
1 small pepper, shredded
½ cup corn kernels with liquid
1 cup cooked tomatoes
3 cups chicken broth (canned)
1 teaspoon salt
⅛ teaspoon dried thyme

Behind the Scenes — Shred both the green pepper and cooked ham into fine shreds julienne. Mince the onions.

Before the Guests — Melt the butter in the blazer pan of the chafing dish. Add ham, pepper and onion and sauté until ham begins to brown. Add remaining ingredients. Heat together until blended into a smooth soup. Serves 4 to 6.

Tray-Maid	*Menu*
1) butter	Ham and Chicken Gumbo
2) ham, shredded	Cornbread Sticks
3) pepper, shredded	Citrus Salad—Cream Dressing
4) onions, minced	Blackberry Pie
5) corn kernels with liquid	Coffee
6) tomatoes, cooked	
7) chicken broth	
8) salt	
9) thyme	

Herb Broth with Cheese

¼ cup finely minced green onion tops or chives
½ cup finely minced greens of watercress, parsley, or fresh dill (if available)
1 leaf fresh basil
1 cup shredded celery stalks and leaves
¼ teaspoon minced fresh tarragon (or "pinch" of dried tarragon)

2 cans concentrated chicken broth
water (to make 1 quart of liquid)
2 tablespoons butter
salt to taste
dash of cayenne pepper
⅛ teaspoon nutmeg
⅓ cup American white wine
toast
grated cheese

Behind the Scenes — Mince the greens quite fine, adding tarragon and basil if they are to be used.

Before the Guests — Place in blazer pan of chafing dish butter, minced greens, shredded celery, seasonings and chicken broth (with enough water added to make a quart of liquid). Simmer over flame about 10 minutes or until greens and celery are cooked. Add wine. Reheat. Place freshly-made toast in bottom of 6 soup bowls. Serve soup and pass grated cheese to be sprinkled over the top. Serves 6.

Tray-Maid	*Menu*
1) water	Herb Broth with Cheese
2) onion	Shrimp Salad
3) minced herbs, watercress, shredded celery	Fig Pudding Hard Sauce
4) butter	Coffee
5) chicken broth	
6) cayenne, nutmeg, salt	
7) wine	
8) cheese	
9) toast	

French Tomato Crème

　1 tablespoon minced onion
　1 clove garlic
　½ teaspoon salt
　2 cups cooked tomatoes
　4 tablespoons butter
　2 tablespoons flour
　2 cups chicken stock
　¾ cup cream
　2 teaspoons minced chives
　1 fresh tomato (optional)

Behind the Scenes — Mince the onion. Mince garlic, then add salt and mash together (using flat side of knife) until garlic is completely dissolved. Rub cooked tomatoes through a strainer. Mince chives.

Before the Guests — Melt butter in blazer pan of chafing dish. Add flour and mix to smooth paste. Add onion, garlic, tomato pulp. Stir until quite thick and smooth. Add chicken soup. Continue cooking until steaming hot. Stir in cream. Add chives. (If a good-flavored fresh tomato is available have it skinned and minced fine ready to add at the last moment. This returns a distinctive fresh flavor to the soup. Serves 4.

Tray-Maid	*Menu*
1) butter	French Tomato Crème
2) flour	Finger Rolls
3) onion and garlic	Salmon Salad with Mayonnaise
4) tomato	and Fresh Dill
5) chicken soup	Pineapple Cheese Cake
6) cream	Coffee
7) chives	
8) fresh tomato (optional)	

Crème Champignon

¼ pound mushrooms
½ medium-sized onion, sliced
2 tablespoons butter
2 tablespoons flour
2 cups chicken stock (home-made or canned)
½ cup light cream or top milk
½ teaspoon salt
¼ teaspoon pepper
¼ teaspoon nutmeg

Behind the Scenes — Wash and slice mushrooms. Slice onion. Measure butter and flour. Place chicken stock in measuring cup. Measure cream. Prepare salad and store in refrigerator until ready to serve.

Before the Guests — Melt butter in blazer pan of chafing dish. Add mushrooms and onion. Sauté for 5 minutes. Blend in flour. Add stock and cream. Season. Heat gently until very hot. Serves 4 to 6.

Tray-Maid	*Menu*
1) mushrooms, sliced	Crème Champignon
2) onion, sliced	Crackers
3) butter, measured out on waxed paper	Egg Salad in Tomato Cups
4) flour	Lemon Sherbet Small Cookies
5) chicken stock in measuring cup	Coffee
6) cream	
7) seasonings—check ingredients	

Be Your Own Author

B.Y.O.A.

CHAPTER THREE

SERVING FOUR TO SIX

Here is the ideal number of guests for a chafing dish cook. Enough to challenge the best you've got, but not enough to create diversions which might cost you their attention. These dishes come straight from heaven—flown in by four to six cherubim.

Flaming Shrimp

2 pounds raw shrimp, shelled
   and cleaned, or 3 eight-
   ounce cans of shrimp
¼ cup sweet butter
½ clove garlic
1 teaspoon minced onion

dash of nutmeg or mace
¼ cup applejack or apple brandy
¾ cup cider
¾ cup heavy cream
chives or parsley

Behind the Scenes — Clean shrimp before guests arrive. Remove sand line. Stick ½ clove garlic on toothpick; it will be easy to discard. Mince onion and place on square of waxed paper; also the chives or parsley. Measure out both brandy and cider into glasses and stand these in containers of hot water.

Before the Guests — Melt butter in blazer pan of chafing dish, add garlic and minced onion. Sauté shrimp in this mixture 5 minutes. Discard garlic and pour heated applejack over shrimp. Ignite and baste shrimp with flaming liquor. When flame dies down, pour hot cider over shrimp. Simmer 3 minutes. Add cream and nutmeg or mace, blend thoroughly. Season to taste and thicken slightly with flour blended with water if desired. Simmer until heated. Serves 4 when the remainder of meal is not heavy and the shrimps serve as bulk. This can be stretched to serve 6 or 8 if accompanied by rice or noodles.

Tray-Maid	*Menu*
1) shrimp, shelled and cleaned	Avocado Halves
2) ½ stick sweet butter	piled high with Jellied Madrilene
3) garlic on toothpick	With Lemon Juice and
4) onion, minced, on waxed paper	Mint Leaves
5) applejack or apple brandy	Flaming Shrimp
6) cider	Potato Chips Stuffed Celery
7) cream	Pastry Coffee
8) nutmeg or mace	
9) salt and pepper grinders	
10) garnish of chives or parsley	

Creamed Prawns (Shrimp) in Spinach Ring

2 dozen raw shrimp
4 tablespoons butter
1 bay leaf
1 tablespoon vinegar
¼ cup water

1 clove garlic
½ teaspoon quick-cooking tapioca
1 pint light cream
¾ cup catsup

Behind the Scenes — Shell the raw shrimp and remove sand line. Prepare a spinach ring. Keep it hot until serving time by placing mold in shallow pan of hot water.
Just a note about using quick-cooking tapioca to thicken a sauce. It is a most delicate thickening and never lumps; needs no beforehand mixing with liquid.

Before the Guests — Melt butter in blazer pan of chafing dish. Add cleaned shrimp, garlic, bay leaf, vinegar and water. Cover and simmer until shrimp turn pink and are cooked to your taste. Use a slotted spoon and remove shrimp to warm bowl; cover and keep warm. Discard garlic and bay leaf; add tapioca and cream. Cook together until richly creamy. Then gradually stir in the catsup. Add the shrimp. Reheat. Turn out the ring of spinach onto serving platter. Fill center with creamed shrimp. Serves 4 to 6.

Tray-Maid	*Menu*

1) butter
2) cooked shrimp
3) shrimp liquor
4) butter, measured out
5) garlic halved
6) vinegar
7) cream
8) water
9) catsup
10) tapioca
11) bay leaf

Tomato Juice Cocktail with
Whole Wheat Crackers
Prawns in Spinach Ring
Potato Chips
Fresh Fruit Salad
Coffee

Mushroom and Artichoke Hearts Gourmet

2 tablespoons butter or margarine
2 ounce can chopped mush-
rooms
1 tablespoon cornstarch
2 tablespoons California sherry
½ cup light cream
½ teaspoon salt

½ teaspoon onion salt
pepper (cayenne or a dash of
Tabasco)
1 pound can or jar artichoke
hearts
juice of 1 lemon
1 pound chicken liver sausage

Behind the Scenes — Measure out butter. Open tin of mushrooms. Mix cornstarch with liquid from mushrooms. Open artichokes and rinse well; then cut in halves lengthwise. Purchase liver sausage in one piece. Remove skin. Cut into halves, then cut each half into 4 wedges.

Before the Guests — Melt butter in blazer pan. Add mushrooms and sauté lightly. Add mushroom liquid stirred well with the cornstarch. Stir over flame until rich and creamy. Remove from flame. Add cream, sherry, salt, onion salt, and pepper. Mix well, using a wooden spoon or silver fork. Mix in lemon juice, then add artichokes and return to flame. Next arrange wedges of liver sausage around edge of pan. Cover and allow sauce to simmer up into artichokes and liver sausage until all is piping hot. On the side have a double boiler of brown or wild rice keeping hot (prepared long before the dining hour). Arrange a ring of rice on serving plates; fill each with mushroom-artichoke mixture and crown with wedge of liver sausage. For garnish use watercress, parsley or chicory. Serve at once. Serves 4 to 6.

Tray-Maid	*Menu*
1) butter, measured out	Antipasto
2) cornstarch with liquid	Mushroom-Artichoke Hearts
3) mushrooms drained of liquid	Gourmet
4) artichokes drained of liquid	Steamed Brown or Wild Rice
5) liver sausage cut for serving	Stewed Apple Compote
6) garnish	Small Cookies
7) cream	Coffee
8) sherry	
9) seasonings	
10) lemon juice	

Mushrooms with Ham

2 pounds fresh mushrooms
1 pound boiled ham, thinly sliced
4 tablespoons butter
juice of 1 lemon
dash of cayenne or Tabasco

1 tablespoon Worcestershire sauce
1 cup hollandaise sauce
1 tablespoon Smithfield Ham Paste, if desired
watercress

Behind the Scenes — Wash mushrooms, remove and slice stems; cut mushrooms in halves or slices, or (if small) leave whole. Hollandaise sauce may be made at home and kept hot in top of double boiler; or, today, very excellent hollandaise sauce may be bought in jars to be heated over hot water before serving, either in a jar or in a serving pan which can be kept hot. This latter sauce may sometimes need the lift of a little lemon juice or wine vinegar, or a touch of Tabasco. Ham paste may be added, if desired.

Before the Guests — Melt butter in blazer pan of chafing dish, add ham and heat through. Turn into heated earthenware (or pyrex) serving dish to keep hot while preparing mushrooms. Turn mushrooms into blazer pan. If necessary (and this depends upon amount of fat that may or may not have been on ham) add extra butter. Sauté the mushrooms until cooked through, stirring to hasten cooking. Add lemon juice and seasonings; turn mushrooms until all are seasoned.

To serve, divide ham between six serving plates, top each serving of ham with mushrooms and then mask the mushrooms in prepared hollandaise. Garnish with watercress. Serves 6.

Tray-Maid	*Menu*
1) mushrooms—cleaned, stemmed, sliced	Cooled Spiced Tomato or Vegetable Juice
2) ham, sliced	Mushrooms with Ham
3) butter, measured out	French Bread or Pumpernickel
4) lemon juice	Sweet Butter
5) cayenne or Tabasco	Watercress and Orange
6) Worcestershire sauce	or Grapefruit Salad
7) hollandaise sauce over hot water	Pastry or Cookies
8) watercress	Coffee

Clams and Bacon

½ pound bacon, sliced thin
4 dozen soft clams
salt and pepper
1 egg
1 tablespoon water
fine bread crumbs
toast
lemon slices

Behind the Scenes — Cut the stringy parts from clams. Drain well. Mix egg with butter. Place bread crumbs on waxed paper.

Before the Guests — Season clams with a little salt and pepper. Beat egg and water. Dip clams into egg, then into crumbs. Fry bacon in blazer pan of chafing dish over open flame until curled and crisp. Remove and keep hot. Fry clams to a nice brown in the drippings that remain in pan. Serve on toast with bacon and lemon. Corn custard baked in individual ramekins is a pleasant accompaniment. These can be baked before the guests arrive and will keep warm if placed in a pan of warm water and covered with a cloth. Serves 4 to 6.

Pour clam juice into bottom pan of chafing dish; heat; serve in small cups with lemon slices on side.

Tray-Maid	*Menu*
1) prepared clams	Cold Borscht with Sour Cream
2) egg and water in dish	and Chives
3) clam juice	Clams and Bacon
4) bread crumbs	Hard Rolls Corn Custard
5) bacon	Wilted Lettuce Salad
6) seasonings	Fresh Grapes and Brownies
7) lemon	Coffee
8) bread for toasting	

Turtle Maryland

2 cups cooked (or canned) turtle meat
4 tablespoons sweet butter
2 tablespoons brandy
3 eggs, hard-cooked
½ cup fish stock or chicken broth
cayenne or Tabasco sauce
½ teaspoon garlic salt (or onion salt)
¼ cup American sherry
3 cups prepared Spanish rice

Behind the Scenes — Cut turtle meat (terrapin) into neat pieces. Prepare Spanish rice (1 cup rice cooked with tomato juice, green pepper, garlic and bacon drippings). Place in double boiler over hot water until time to serve. Cook eggs. Cool. Remove yolks and mash them with 2 tablespoons of the butter. Slice the egg white into circles.

Before the Guests — Melt half the butter in blazer pan of chafing dish, directly over the flame; add turtle meat and brandy. Stir gently 3 to 4 minutes (with silver fork, until heated through). Add prepared egg yolk and butter. Add stock or broth, garlic salt, cayenne or Tabasco. Stir until sauce is thickened. Add sherry. Quickly reheat. Serve beside the Spanish rice with rings of egg white for garnish. Serves 4 to 6.

Tray-Maid	*Menu*
1) turtle meat cut in neat pieces	Chilled Melon with Lime Juice
2) butter measured out	Turtle Maryland
3) brandy	with
4) sherry	Spanish Rice
5) stock	Tossed Salad
6) egg yolks mashed with butter	Washington Pie
7) egg whites, sliced thinly	Coffee
8) seasonings—see ingredients	
9) Spanish rice in double boiler over hot water	

Scrambled Eggs with Asparagus Tips

½ to 1 cup asparagus tips (fresh
  or frozen)
6 eggs
½ teaspoon salt
2 teaspoons butter
¼ teaspoon pepper

Behind the Scenes — Prepare asparagus. Have eggs broken into bowl ready for cooking.

Before the Guests — Beat eggs slightly with a fork. Melt butter in blazer pan of chafing dish over open flame. Turn in eggs, and before they are quite set season with salt and pepper to taste and then add the asparagus tips. Gently stir the mixture until eggs are set. Serve on dainty slices of buttered toast with French-fried onion rings (canned or home fried— heated in lower pan of chafing dish beforehand and kept hot while eggs are cooking).

Tray-Maid	*Menu*
1) eggs broken into bowl	Molded Perfection Salad
2) onion rings (from can) or pre-cooked	Scrambled Eggs with Asparagus Tips
3) asparagus	Onion Rings
4) butter measured on waxed paper	French Bread
5) seasonings	Chocolate Roll
	Coffee

French Jelly Omelet

> 5 eggs
> 5 tablespoons water
> 1 teaspoon salt
> ⅛ teaspoon pepper
> 2 tablespoons butter or marga-
>   rine
>   tart grape or currant jelly

Behind the Scenes — Break eggs into mixing bowl; add water, salt and pepper. To make jelly easy to spread, beat up with fork.

Before the Guests — Mix eggs in bowl just sufficiently to blend. Avoid foaminess. Heat batter in blazer pan of chafing dish just hot enough to sizzle a drop of water. Pour egg mixture in blazer pan and reduce heat by closing off part of the blaze. As the mixture at the edges begins to thicken, draw the cooked portions with a fork toward the center so that the uncooked portions flow to the bottom. Tilt pan as it is necessary to hasten flow of uncooked eggs. Do not stir. When eggs no longer flow and surface is still moist, increase heat to brown bottom quickly. Carefully loosen edge. Spread half of top with jelly. Fold in half or roll. Total cooking time 5 to 8 minutes. Serves 4.

Tray-Maid	*Menu*
1) bowl with eggs and seasonings	Clear Consommé
2) butter	Cocktail Sausages
3) jelly	Jelly Omelet
4) cocktail sausages heated in lower pan of chafing dish and kept hot on the side	Salted Rolls
	Pistachio Ice Cream
	Coffee

Anchovy-Stuffed Eggs

4 to 6 hard-cooked eggs
anchovy paste to taste
½ teaspoon rich prepared mustard
¼ teaspoon curry powder
1 tablespoon cornstarch
⅛ teaspoon powdered ginger

1 cup chicken broth (from 10½-ounce tin)
¼ cup heavy cream
1 egg yolk
1 tablespoon butter or margarine
½ pound very thin noodles, cooked
1 tablespoon minced parsley

Behind the Scenes — Cut hard-cooked eggs in halves lengthwise. Remove yolks and reserve one yolk for garnishing. Mash remaining yolks and add anchovy paste, mustard and curry powder to taste. (Add a few drops of milk or cream if yolks need additional moisture.) When yolk mixture is creamy, but not wet, refill hollows of egg whites.

Cook noodles in boiling salted water. Drain and keep hot in top of double boiler over hot water. Mince parsley.

Before the Guests — Mix cornstarch and ginger with broth in blazer pan in chafing dish until smooth. Place over flame and stir until smooth and *clear*. Add cream. Mix and remove from over flame. Add raw egg yolk and mix well. Add butter. Place blazer pan over hot water and when piping hot arrange eggs in sauce. Cover and heat through.

To Serve: Add minced parsley to noodles. Serve a mound of noodles on individual serving plate; make a little hollow in center and serve two halves of eggs in each serving. Cover with sauce. Rub egg yolk through a sieve over top of each serving. Serves 4 to 6.

Tray-Maid	*Menu*
1) stuffed eggs	Tossed Green Salad with
2) cornstarch	Bleu Cheese Dressing
3) broth	Anchovy-Stuffed Eggs
4) cream	In Bechamel Sauce
5) egg yolk	with
6) spice	Parsley Noodles
7) butter	Chocolate Bread Pudding
8) noodles over hot water	with Whipped Cream
9) minced parsley	Coffee

Fondue Neuchâteloise

½ lb. the best Swiss cheese, shredded or finely cut

1½ tablespoons flour

1 clove fresh garlic

1 cup of any light dry white wine of the Rhine, Riesling or Chablis types

salt, pepper, nutmeg to taste.

1 loaf French or other bread with a hard crust (or at least four hard rolls), cut into bite-size pieces, each of which must have at least one side of crust.

(Optional) 3 tablespoons Kirschwasser or 2 tablespoons of any non-sweetened fruit brandy such as applejack, slivovitz, cognac, etc., or light rum.

Behind the Scenes — There is little beforehand preparation. Shred the cheese and mix well with the flour.

Before the Guests — Rub the blazer pan of your chafing dish thoroughly with garlic. Pour in the wine and set over very slow fire. When the wine is heated to the point when air bubbles rise to the surface (*never* to the boiling point), stir with a fork and add the cheese by handfuls, each handful to be completely dissolved before another one is added.

Keep stirring until the mixture starts bubbling lightly. At this point add a little salt and pepper and a dash of nutmeg (optional). Finally add and thoroughly stir in the Kirschwasser (or other brandy). Reduce flame and keep fondue hot—serving begins at once.

Tray-Maid

1) shredded cheese mixed with flour, placed on large square waxed paper.
2) clove of garlic, cut into halves
3) bottle of wine
4) French bread

Huîtres en Coquilles

4 tablespoons butter	1 tablespoon grated onion
½ pint heavy cream	1 tablespoon minced parsley
salt	8 drops celery extract
3 egg yolks	25 large oysters
1 tablespoon flour	cayenne

Behind the Scenes — Be sure to drain oysters (saving the liquid, of course) and run your fingers carefully through the oysters to remove bits of shell.

Before the Guests — Melt 3 tablespoons of the butter in the blazer pan of the chafing dish, then add flour. When blended and smooth, add cream, oyster liquid, grated onion, celery extract, salt to taste and a dash of cayenne. Stir until sauce becomes creamy and the flour is well cooked. Then place blazer pan over hot water and add the egg yolks, stirring well as you add to prevent lumping. Stir over hot water until well blended. Cover and set aside to keep warm. Empty water from lower pan of chafing dish. Place it over flame. In it melt the remaining 1 tablespoon of butter. Add oysters and sauté until cooked through. Add minced parsley. Serve beside waffles, then cover with sauce. Serves 4 to 6.

Tray-Maid	*Menu*
1) butter measured out onto neat square waxed paper	Pineapple and Mint Fruit Cup
	Waffles
2) cream	Huîtres En Coquilles
3) egg yolks, separated	Celery Curls Radish Roses
4) onion, grated or finely minced	Petit Fours
5) oysters, drained, clear of shells	Coffee
6) oyster liquid, separate	
7) waffle batter in pitcher	
8) seasonings	
9) flour	
10) parsley	
11) celery extract	

Curried Lobster

1 tablespoon butter
1 tart apple, minced
curry powder to taste
1 onion, minced
1 tablespoon cornstarch
½ pint cream
3 to 4 pound live lobster

Behind the Scenes — Either cook the lobster and cut meat neatly or use 1 to 2 cans lobster meat ready for use. Mince apple and onion; sprinkle with a little lemon juice to keep apple from turning brown. Measure cornstarch into measuring cup, then gradually add enough cream to make a liquid.

Before the Guests — Melt butter in blazer pan of chafing dish. Add onion and apple and cook thoroughly. Sprinkle with curry powder, according to taste, from a teaspoon to a tablespoonful. Add cornstarch mixed with cream. Add any remaining cream. Stir until sauce is rich and creamy. (Taste to be sure cornstarch is well cooked, then add the lobster cut in pieces.) Heat well. Serve with plain boiled rice and accompaniments.

Tray-Maid	*Menu*
1) cooked or canned lobster	Fresh Fruit Cup
2) apple and onion, ready minced	Lobster Curry
3) cornstarch in cream	with
4) butter	Boiled Rice and
5) leftover cream from half pint	Salted Nuts Chutney
6) rice boiled over hot water	Shredded Coconut
7) curry powder	Raisins
(Note: curry extras are on dining or buffet table.)	Steamed Pudding
	Hard Sauce
	Coffee

Creamed Lobster in Fragrant Potato Cases

2 tablespoons butter
2 tablespoons cake flour
1 cup top milk
1 bay leaf
⅛ teaspoon celery seeds
½ teaspoon salt
⅛ teaspoon pepper

1 egg, beaten with tablespoon water
2 cups cooked or canned lobster meat
6 potato cases
parsley or watercress

Behind the Scenes — If fresh lobster is used, it must be boiled, cooled, removed from shell and cut into pieces. Wash parsley or watercress and crisp. *To prepare potato cases:* use 3 cups mashed potatoes, prepared and seasoned as usual. Add grated rind of one lemon (the yellow, never the bitter white part) and a dash of grated nutmeg or mace. Shape into six oblong patties and press a hollow into center of each. Brush with prepared egg. Place on greased tray; heat in 350° F. (or cooler) oven shortly before serving time. Allow cases to warm slowly while guests are arriving and during preparation of lobster.

Before the Guests — Melt butter in blazer pan of chafing dish. Add flour, mix smoothly. Add milk gradually, followed by bay leaf and celery seeds. Stir to creamy sauce. Add salt, pepper and remaining egg (left over from brushing of potato cases). Add lobster. Stir gently to keep lobster in fairly large pieces. Place pan over hot water and heat lobster through. Remove bay leaf. Bring potato cases from oven piping hot and fill with prepared lobster. Garnish with sprigs of parsley or watercress.

Tray-Maid	*Menu*
1) butter, measured onto neat square of paper	Carrot-Celery-Olive Nibbles
2) flour, also measured as above	Creamed Lobster in Fragrant Potato Cases
3) milk, measured out	Tossed Green Salad
4) seasonings—check ingredients	Apple Pie and Cheese
5) egg	Coffee
6) lobster, cooked and cut into bite-sized pieces	
7) parsley or watercress	

Deviled Lobster

3 tablespoons butter
1 teaspoon curry powder
2 tablespoons fine dry crumbs
1 teaspoon Worcestershire sauce
1 tablespoon vinegar
1 teaspoon mustard

salt
cayenne
graham toast
4 live lobsters (1½ pounds each)
  or 2 to 3 pounds lobster meat
  (prepared)

Behind the Scenes — Boil lobster; when cold extract meat and cut into moderately sized pieces. Heat shoestring potatoes in lower pan of chafing dish. Keep hot while preparing lobster.

Before the Guests — Put in blazer pan of chafing dish, over open flame, the butter, curry powder and crumbs. Mix well; then add Worcestershire sauce, vinegar, mustard, salt and cayenne to taste. When well blended, add lobster. Stir constantly. When lobster is well dressed with the sauce and well heated through, serve on either graham toast or thin slices of buttered graham bread. Serves 4.

Tray-Maid	*Menu*

1) cooked lobster
2) seasonings, check ingredients
3) shoestring potatoes
4) toast
5) butter
6) crumbs
7) vinegar
8) Worcestershire

Picture Salad of Cooked
Vegetables
Deviled Lobster
Shoestring Potatoes
Apricot Tapioca or
Strawberry Shortcake
Coffee

Tongue with Sauce Dijon

1 can or jar of pork, veal, or lamb tongue (about 12 ounces)
1 tablespoon drippings
1 small onion, thinly sliced
½ teaspoon Maggi
6 to 8 small potatoes, cooked in their jackets
freshly ground pepper
2 eggs hard-cooked
½ cup grape or currant jelly
4 tablespoons rich prepared mustard
2 tablespoons grated onion

Behind the Scenes — Open tin of tongue; if necessary, slice each tongue lengthwise into thick pieces. Scrub 6 to 8 very small potatoes and boil in their jackets until tender. Drain. Cut into halves. Boil 2 eggs along with the potatoes. When cool, shell and cut into halves or quarters. To make *Sauce Dijon:* mix jelly, mustard and grated onion. Heat gently until jelly is softened. Taste and add extra mustard or onion, as desired, to satisfy your taste.

Before the Guests — Remove fat from around meat and transfer to blazer pan of chafing dish. Add drippings. Heat over flame, add the sliced onion and sauté 2 to 3 minutes. Add Maggi, then tongue, placing it neatly in the pan. Arrange the potatoes cut side down around outer rim of pan. Grind black pepper over surface. Cover; cook 3 to 4 minutes to allow sauce to simmer into meat and potatoes. Then cook additional 5 minutes, basting with sauce in bottom of pan. At this point potatoes may be removed to serving dish if desired to be sprinkled with chopped parsley, then covered to keep warm. Place eggs in blazer pan (which is still over the flame) then pour Sauce Dijon in a ribbon over top of meat and eggs. Cover. Heat well. Serve piping hot. Serves 4.

Tray-Maid

1) tongue, properly cut
2) drippings, measured out
3) onion, sliced and separated into rings
4) Maggi
5) cooked potatoes, halved
6) eggs, hard-cooked, quartered
7) pepper grinder
8) Sauce Dijon

Menu

Chilled Grapefruit
Tongue with Sauce Dijon
Cole Slaw with Vinegar Dressing
Cheese and Crackers
Coffee

Shad Roe with Wine Sauce

2 to 4 pair shad roe (depending upon size)
6 tablespoons butter
1 small onion, minced
1 tablespoon vinegar
1 tablespoon fine bread crumbs
juice of 1 lemon
½ teaspoon minced parsley
1 cup white wine
½ teaspoon sugar
salt and pepper
1 teaspoon paprika
toast points
lime quarter

Behind the Scenes — Roe is always best when pre-cooked in simmering salted water about 15 minutes. Separate after cooking; they are easier to handle in the chafing dish.

Before the Guests — Melt butter in blazer pan of chafing dish. Add onion and sauté until golden. Add remaining ingredients except roe and bring to a simmer. Taste and adjust seasoning at this point to assure yourself the sauce is perfect. Then add roe and cook in slowly bubbling sauce about 10 minutes. Serve on buttered toast points with a quarter of lime for each serving. Serve with whole grain hominy (which can be bought in cans) or boiled rice, noodles or scalloped potatoes—any of which may be prepared long before the supper hour, kept hot in the oven or over hot water. Serves 4 to 6.

Tray-Maid

1) shad roe, pre-cooked and separated
2) butter, measured out
3) onion, minced
4) vinegar
5) wine
6) crumbs, measured out
7) parsley, minced
8) lemon juice, squeezed
9) seasonings—check ingredients
10) bread for toast or toast
11) lime

Menu

Tomato Stuffed with
Vegetable Salad
Shad Roe in Wine Sauce
Hominy
Fruit Pie   Coffee

Danish Meat Balls with Sour Cream Sauce

2 slices whole wheat or rye bread
1 pound ground beef
2 large onions, finely minced
½ teaspoon salt
    pepper
1 egg
    fine cracker or bread crumbs

4 tablespoons butter or margarine
1 onion, thinly sliced, separated into rings
2 tablespoons Worcestershire sauce
½ cup sour cream
¼ teaspoon ground nutmeg

Behind the Scenes — Soak the bread in cold water, then press out to dryness between your hands. "Fluff" this moist bread and add to the meat. Add minced onion, salt, pepper, egg. Mix well. Shape into balls, each about 1½ to 2 inches in diameter. This will make about 2 dozen balls. Roll in the fine dry crumbs. Mix sour cream with nutmeg.

Before the Guests — Melt butter (or drippings) in blazer pan of chafing dish. Add onion rings and sauté to delicate brown. Add Worcestershire sauce. Then fill the pan with the meat balls. Turn to brown on all sides. Pile the browned balls to one side and keep adding more until all are cooked. Then pour the sour cream (which has been mixed beforehand with nutmeg) in a neat ribbon, back and forth across top of meat balls. Serve at once. Serves 4 to 6.

Tray-Maid	*Menu*
1) meat balls, shaped and crumbed	Hors d'Oeuvres
2) onion, sliced and separated into rings	Danish Meat Balls with Sour Cream Sauce
3) butter, measured out	Boiled New Potatoes with Parsley Butter
4) Worcestershire sauce	Tomato and Cucumber Salad
5) sour cream mixed with nutmeg	Baked Apples
	Coffee

Chili Balls

¾ pound ground beef
½ pound ground veal
1 teaspoon chili powder
1 cup fine crumbs
1 tablespoon flour
2 onions, finely minced
1 teaspoon celery salt
4 tablespoons butter **or drip-**
  pings

1 clove garlic
½ teaspoon salt
1 bay leaf, finely crumbled
1 teaspoon lemon juice
2 tablespoons water
½ can (10½-ounce size) **tomato**
  soup
  minced parsley
1 large can kidney beans, heated

Behind the Scenes — Mix beef, veal, chili powder, ½ cup of fine crumbs, flour, 1 onion finely minced and celery salt. When well mixed, shape into balls 1 ½ to 2 inches in diameter. Roll in the remaining half cup of crumbs; arrange on plate. Heat the kidney beans and place over hot water to stay hot. (Season with additional chili powder, if desired.) Prepare the garlic ahead of time, too. Mince it fine on a bread board, then add salt and rub it into the garlic with flat side of a knife until all particles of garlic disappear.

Before the Guests — Melt butter or drippings in blazer pan of chafing dish. Add the other onion and garlic. Fry the balls in this to golden brown. When all are cooked, either remove from pan to serving dish to keep hot or pile onto one side of pan. Add bay leaf, lemon juice, water, and tomato soup. Cover and simmer until well blended. Baste the meat balls in the pan or pour over those in serving dish. Serve with heated kidney beans. Top with minced parsley. Serves 4 to 6.

Tray-Maid

1) meat balls, shaped and
     crumbed
2) kidney beans, heated and
     kept hot over hot water
3) butter, measured out
4) onion
5) garlic paste with salt
6) bay leaf
7) lemon juice
8) tomato soup, measured out
9) parsley, minced
10) water

Menu

Sliced Pepper, Celery and
Cucumber Cut Into Sticks
Chili Balls with
Kidney Beans
Hot Corn Sticks
Cheese Cake
Coffee

Rabbit with Beer (Welsh Rarebit)

1 pound good American
    cheese
2 tablespoons butter
1 cup light beer
1 egg
    dash of cayenne
1 tablespoon dry mustard
½ teaspoon Worcestershire sauce
    salt

Behind the Scenes — Cut cheese into small pieces.

Before the Guests — Melt butter in blazer pan of chafing dish. Add cheese and melt very slowly. Mix seasoning in cup with a tablespoon of beer, add egg and beat together. As the cheese melts, add the beer, a little at a time, stopping when the mixture reaches the consistency of thick cream. Stir constantly in the same direction. The melting and stirring-in of the beer should take at least half an hour. Be careful that it never bubbles. When perfectly smooth, stir in the egg. The cheese mixture should be hot enough so that the egg thickens it slightly. Pour over toasted bread on very hot plates. Serves 4 to 6.

Tray-Maid	*Menu*
1) cheese cut fine	Chilled Raw Sauerkrau
2) seasonings—check ingredients	Rabbit on Toast
3) measuring spoons	Tossed Salad
4) egg broken into measuring	Fruit
cup	Coffee
5) beer	

Hungarian Veal Paprika

1½ pounds veal sliced ⅜" thick
½ cup flour
1½ teaspoon salt
freshly ground black pepper
Kitchen Bouquet
½ cup butter or olive oil
¾ tablespoon paprika
½ cup hot water

1 cup light cream or sour cream
1 medium onion, sliced thinly
1 package medium-wide noodles, cooked
½ cup almonds, blanched and shredded
1 tablespoon poppy seeds

Behind the Scenes — If butcher cuts veal too thick flatten it with a mallet or cleaver. Add salt and pepper to flour and rub well into meat. Cut meat into two inch squares. Brush with Kitchen Bouquet. Cook noodles and combine with almonds and poppy seeds. Keep hot over water.

Before the Guests — Heat butter or oil in blazer pan of chafing dish and brown meat well on both sides. Sprinkle paprika over meat and add onion and ½ cup hot water. Cover and simmer 30 minutes or until meat is tender. Stir in cream and allow to bubble up a moment. Serve sauce over hot noodles and place veal on top. Serves 4 liberally.

Tray-Maid

1) veal steak, prepared
2) noodles over hot water
3) butter, measured out
4) onion, thinly sliced
5) paprika
6) cream
7) ½ cup hot water

Menu

Hot Consommé Laced
with Sherry
Veal Paprika with Noodles
Green Salad
Fruit Tart
Coffee

Beef Stroganoff

1½ pounds fillet of beef or the lean part of tenderloin
1½ teaspoons salt
2 teaspoons pepper
3 tablespoons butter

1 tablespoon flour
1 cup consommé
1 scant teaspoon prepared hot mustard
1 onion, sliced
3 tablespoons thick sour cream

Behind the Scenes — Remove all fat and gristle from the meat. Cut it in narrow strips about 2″ long and ½″ thick. Dust the strips of beef with salt and pepper, then set aside at room temperature for two hours.

Before the Guests — Melt 1½ tablespoons of the butter in blazer pan of chafing dish. Add flour and blend. Add the consommé and bring to a boil. Stir in the mustard. Brown the strips of meat very quickly with the sliced onion in the remaining 1½ tablespoon butter, using lower part of chafing dish. Have the sour cream at room temperature. Add it to the mustard sauce and boil up once. Discard onion. Then add meat to the sauce. Cover the pan and keep hot for 20 minutes, taking care it doesn't boil or even simmer. Set the pan over brisk heat for 3 minutes before serving. Serve immediately. Serves 4 generously.

Tray-Maid

1) prepared beef
2) butter, measured out
3) flour
4) mustard
5) consommé
6) onion
7) sour cream
8) kasha (may be purchased in cans) or boiled rice over hot water

Menu

Tossed Salad
Beef Stroganoff with Kasha or Rice
Hard Rolls
Cucumbers Cut in Sticks
French Pastry
Coffee

Fritadella (Spanish Meat and Egg Hash)

2 tablespoons butter or 2
   strips bacon
bread (dry)
½ teaspoon salt
   dash of pepper
   rind of 1 lemon
½ tablespoon beef essence

1 onion, minced
1½ to 2 cups cooked ground
   meat
   grated nutmeg
¼ cup hot water
2 eggs

Behind the Scenes — Put through meat grinder enough cooked meat (of any kind) with onion to make 1½ to 2 cups when ground. Finish grinding with 3 slices dry bread or 6 crackers. Mix all well but lightly. Season with salt and pepper, grated nutmeg and grated rind of lemon. Heat can of sweet potatoes in bottom of chafing dish pan and keep hot until serving time. Sprinkle with sugar and dot with butter.

Before the Guests — Put butter or bacon cut small in blazer pan of chafing dish. Cook for about 2 minutes, then add meat. Cook until meat begins to brown on bottom, then add the hot water in which meat essence has been dissolved. Simmer until well heated and seasoned through. Stir in the eggs one at a time and cook just long enough to set. Serve with potatoes, all piping hot. Serves 4 to 6.

Tray-Maid	*Menu*
1) ground meat	Cheese Puffs
2) 2 eggs	Fritadella
3) water with essence dissolved in it	with
	Sweet Potatoes
4) can of sweet potatoes emptied into lower pan of chafing dish	Raw Carrot and
	White Turnip Julienne
	Apple Pan Dowdy
5) butter, measured out	Coffee
6) sugar	

Veal Steak Italienne

1 pound veal steak, sliced very
    thin
4 tomatoes
¼ pound mozzarella cheese
⅛ teaspoon orégano
½ teaspoon salt
⅛ teaspoon pepper or a dash of
    cayenne
1 egg, beaten with 1 tablespoon
    water
½ cup bread crumbs
2 tablespoons parsley, minced
    olive or salad oil or butter

Behind the Scenes — Cut veal into serving pieces. Combine parsley with bread crumbs. Dip veal pieces into crumbs, then into egg, and again into crumbs. Slice cheese. Skim and slice tomatoes.

Before the Guests — Place just enough oil in blazer pan of chafing dish to cover bottom. Brown veal pieces slowly on both sides. Pile pieces to one side of pan until all pieces have been browned. Then arrange neatly in pan and place the tomato slices over top. Add seasonings and cover. Cook slowly for ten minutes. Remove cover and arrange cheese in neat pattern over tomato slices. Cover and cook 10 minutes longer or until cheese is melted. Serve with potato patties, heated beforehand in bottom pan of chafing dish. (These can now be purchased quick-frozen, if desired.) Serves 4 to 6.

Tray-Maid	*Menu*
1) veal slices, crumbed	Olives in Aspic
2) tomatoes, sliced	Veal Steak Italienne
3) cheese, sliced	Potato Patties
4) seasoning—check ingredients	Tossed Green Salad
5) olive oil	Biscuit Tortoni
	Coffee

Sherried Ham and Sweetbreads

1 pair sweetbreads
2 slices boiled ham ¼ inch
   thick
½ pound mushrooms
4 tablespoons butter

½ cup heavy cream
½ cup sherry
¼ teaspoon pepper
½ teaspoon salt
   toast triangles

Behind the Scenes — Prepare sweetbreads; wash and let stand in cold water 20 minutes. Drain; plunge into boiling water with 2 tablespoons vinegar and 2 teaspoons salt. Cover and simmer 30 minutes. Plunge into cold water. Drain; remove fat, tissue and membrane. Cut in cubes. Wash and slice mushrooms.

Before the Guests — Melt butter in blazer pan of chafing dish. Sauté ham slices 3 minutes. Remove and keep hot. Sauté mushrooms 5 minutes in same butter. Add sweetbread cubes and cook slowly for 10 minutes, tossing frequently. Add cream and seasonings. Heat thoroughly. Just before removing from flame add wine. Arrange a piece of ham on a toast triangle and cover with the mushroom-sweetbread mixture. Sweet potatoes may be served with this dish. If desired, use canned sweets and heat in bottom pan of chafing dish before guests arrive. Serve together, piping hot. Serves 4 to 6.

Tray-Maid

1) sweetbreads, prepared and
   cubed
2) ham, cut in serving pieces
3) mushrooms, sliced
4) cream
5) butter, measured out on
   waxed paper
6) sherry
7) bread for toast
8) salt and pepper

Menu

Spiced Vegetable Juice
Sherried Ham and Sweetbreads
Sweet Potatoes
Head Lettuce with
Tart French Dressing
Fruit Ice
Coffee

Veal Birds

1½ pounds veal
3 slices bacon
1 onion, finely minced
1 cup fine bread crumbs
2 tablespoons parsley minced
¼ teaspoon thyme

salt and pepper
flour
Kitchen Bouquet
4 tablespoons butter
½ cup chicken broth (from can or bouillon cubes)
bay leaf

Behind the Scenes — Purchase veal steak or veal cut from the leg in paper-thin pieces (such as you would buy for veal parmigiana). Cut into 12 pieces, each 3½ x 4 inches square. To make a stuffing for these birds: cut bacon to bits and heat until crisp and delicately brown. Remove from heat and add onion, bread crumbs, parsley, thyme, ¼ teaspoon salt and dash of pepper. Mix well. Divide among the 12 squares of veal. Spread over surface, then roll meat with stuffing as you would a jelly roll. Tie into shape or fasten with toothpicks or small skewers. Salt and pepper outside of meat. Brush with Kitchen Bouquet. Sprinkle lightly with flour.

Before the Guests — Melt butter in blazer pan of chafing dish. When it begins to brown add as many veal birds as possible at one time and sauté until brown all over. Add more butter if needed during cooking. When all are brown return to blazer pan. Add chicken broth to cover bottom of pan, add bay leaf, finely crushed. Cook about 20 minutes, basting from time to time. Adding more broth as needed, until birds are well cooked and sauce of desired consistency. Serve with rice or noodles or baked potatoes prepared ahead of time and kept hot. Serves 4 to 6.

Tray-Maid

1) butter
2) veal birds, prepared for cooking
3) chicken broth
4) bay leaf, crushed
5) rice, kept warm over hot water

Menu

Mixed Vegetable Salad with Mayonnaise
Veal Birds
Baked Idaho Potatoes
Floating Island
Coffee

Land of the Sun Liver Patties

      1 pound beef liver
      ½ pound sliced bacon
      1 cup raw grated potatoes
      2 teaspoons salt
      ⅛ teaspoon pepper
      ¼ teaspoon ginger
      1 teaspoon grated onion
      ½ lb. noodles, boiled

Behind the Scenes — Peel and grate potato. Squeeze out excess moisture. Put liver through food chopper. Combine liver with potato, onion and seasonings. Prepare noodles and keep hot until serving time.

Before the Guests — Cook bacon slices in blazer pan of chafing dish. Remove slices when crisp and keep hot. Drop liver mixture by spoonfuls into hot bacon drippings; flatten with spatula; brown on both sides. Serve with crisp bacon slices and with the noodles which were prepared beforehand and kept hot. Serves 4 to 6.

Tray-Maid	*Menu*
1) liver, prepared 2) bacon	Stuffed Celery Land of the Sun Liver Patties with Bacon Poppyseed Noodles Asparagus Vinaigrette Cherry Cobbler Coffee

½ lb. lean pork, coarsely ground
1 green onion
1 small carrot
1 stalk celery
  salt
  pepper
2 live baby lobsters
1 cup chicken bouillon
1 egg
2 tablespoons constarch
2 teaspoons soy sauce
¼ cup water
2 tablespoons olive oil

Behind the Scenes — Mince onion, carrot, celery. Mix vegetables with pork. Season with salt and pepper. Cook the lobsters in boiling water 5 minutes. Cool and remove meat. Cut in fairly large pieces. Blend cornstarch and soy sauce with ¼ cup of water. Beat egg slightly.

Before the Guests — Place oil in blazer pan and heat bouillon and cook slowly for 10 minutes. Raise flame and add egg. Cook 2 minutes, stirring constantly. Add cornstarch-soy sauce mixture and cook 2 more minutes. Keep stirring until sauce thickens. Serve at once with rice. Serves 4.

Tray-Maid	*Menu*
1) oil	Egg Roll
2) lobster	Lobster Cantonese
3) bouillon	Rice
4) egg	Almond Cakes
5) cornstarch-soy sauce mixture	Tea

B.Y.O.A.

B.Y.O.A.

CHAPTER FOUR

SPECIALITÉ OF THE
CHAFING DISH

Here is where the Maestro of the Wooden Spoon sparkles like the Kohinoor under lights! We should warn you, perhaps, that these superlative curries can bring out the East Indian in a man. Suggestion: lay in a supply of turbans and cobra clarinets, just as a hedge.

East Indies Curry (A Basic Curry)

1 pound neck of lamb, cut in 1-
    inch pieces
2 tablespoons butter
2 tablespoons flour
1 apple
1 medium-sized onion
2 shallots
1 clove garlic
1 tomato, skinned
½ small eggplant, peeled
1 stalk celery

1 tablespoon curry powder
1 cup stock
2 teaspoons salt
1 teaspoon pepper
¼ teaspoon crushed bay leaf and
    thyme
    piece of lemon rind
4 tablespoons cooked green peas
6 small pickled onions
2 cups cooked rice

Behind the Scenes — Have butcher bone lamb and cut into pieces. Dredge with flour. Mince apple and all vegetables except pickled onions and peas. Cook peas. Cook rice and keep warm for serving time.

Before the Guests — Melt butter in blazer pan of chafing dish. Brown the dredged lamb pieces on all sides, stirring occasionally for about 6 minutes. Add minced apple and vegetables. Add curry powder and stir well. Add stock, salt, pepper, bay leaf, thyme and lemon rind (remove rind before serving). Stir until well blended. Cover and cook for 15 minutes. Add peas and pickled onions. Cook another 5 minutes. Arrange the hot rice in hot platter; hollow out center and pour curry mixture into center of rice. Serve with six or eight of the condiments listed below. Serves 4.
(Note: This is an authentic curry. To simplify it the shallots, eggplant, peas and pickled onions may be omitted.)

Basic Curry

butter
lamb, dredged in flour
minced apple
minced vegetables
curry powder
stock
seasonings—check ingredients
lemon rind
cooked peas
pickled onions
rice, kept warm

Accompaniments

Choose your accompaniment for East Indies Curry from among the following:

1. chopped peanuts
2. chopped cashew nuts
3. whole almonds
4. chopped pomelo
   (Chinese grapefruit peel)
5. chopped orange peel
6. chopped apples
7. chopped ripe bananas
8. chopped ripe pineapple
9. chopped green peppers
10. chopped fried eggplant
11. chopped dill pickle
12. India relish
13. French fried onions
14. fried onions
15. chopped raw onions
16. Bombay duck
17. chopped ripe olives
18. chopped stuffed olives
19. chopped cucumbers
20. chopped crisp bacon
21. chutney
22. raisins
23. grated fresh coconut
24. chopped egg white
25. chopped egg yolk
26. toasted coconut
27. small pickled onions
28. candied ginger
29. sliced tomatoes
30. brown sugar
31. mangoes
32. tamarind jam
33. dried fish

Hawaiian Lobster Curry

2 lobsters (1½ pounds each)
½ onion, chopped
1 clove garlic, mashed to pulp
1 small piece grated ginger
  root
1½ tablespoons of cornstarch
1½ tablespoons curry powder
1 grated coconut
  salt and pepper to taste

Behind the Scenes — Open and drain coconut. Chop onion and mash garlic. Cook lobsters in boiling salted water for 20 minutes. Drain; open and remove meat. Cut in fairly good-sized pieces. Cook rice and keep warm.

Before the Guests — Melt butter in blazer pan of chafing dish. Sauté onion and garlic until onion is soft but not browned. Blend in cornstarch (mixed to a thin paste with a little of the coconut milk). Add seasonings. Add milk strained from the coconut. Cook, stirring constantly until sauce is rich and creamy. Bring to boiling point, then add grated coconut and lobster meat. Season correctly and serve piping hot.

Tray-Maid	*Menu*
1) minced onion	Mushroom Consommé
2) garlic, mashed	Hawaiian Lobster Curry
3) grated gingeroot	Rice
4) cornstarch, mixed	Tomatoes with Chives
5) grated coconut	Fruit Bowl
6) milk	Coffee
7) curry	
8) salt and pepper	
9) lobster pieces	
10) rice kept warm	
11) butter	

A Delicate Dry Curry

2 large onions, cut into thick
   slices
2 tablespoons butter or margarine
2 cans tuna fish
½ cup raisins
½ pound almonds, blanched
2 tablespoons curry powder
3 cups rice, uncooked

Behind the Scenes — Slice onions into thick slices; open cans of tuna. Cover raisins with boiling water and allow to "plump" for an hour; then drain. Blanch almonds, skin, and cut into halves lengthwise. Wash and boil the rice; keep hot until serving time.

Before the Guests — Melt butter in blazer pan; add onions and sauté until tender. Stir in curry powder. Add tuna (with its oil); add raisins and almonds. Stir with a fork over the flame until piping hot. Add to the hot rice and again mix well but lightly, using a silver fork. Serves 6 to 8.

Tray-Maid	*Menu*
1) butter	Delicate Dry Curry
2) onions, sliced	Pineapple Salad
3) tuna with oil	Crisp Wafers
4) raisins, plumped	Coffee
5) almonds, blanched and halved	Mints
6) rice, kept warm	

Chicken or Turkey Curry, American Style

1 can drained mushrooms (4-ounce size)
¼ cup butter or margarine
¼ cup flour
1 teaspoon salt
1½ cups liquid (broth, mushroom juice, coconut milk or water)
½ cup top milk or cream
2 to 3 cups diced cooked turkey or chicken

½ cup shredded or finely chopped coconut, preferably fresh
1 teaspoon curry powder (more if desired)
½ teaspoon ginger
½ teaspoon celery seed
¼ teaspoon white pepper
4 to 6 cups cooked rice (1½ to 2 cups raw)

Behind the Scenes — Dice the cooked turkey or chicken neatly. Prepare rice and keep warm. Grate or chop the coconut if fresh is used. (Canned Southern-style rice is an excellent substitute.)

Before the Guests — Melt butter in blazer pan of chafing dish. Add mushrooms and brown. Add flour and salt. Stir until blended. Add liquid plus milk or cream. Stir over flame until rich and creamy and thoroughly cooked. Add turkey or chicken, coconut and seasonings. Stir until turkey is heated through, then place over hot water and continue cooking until all ingredients are well flavored. Serve over hot rice. Serves 6 to 8.

Tray-Maid

1) butter
2) diced turkey or chicken
3) mushrooms
4) flour and salt
5) milk or cream, liquid
6) coconut
7) seasonings

Menu

Serve with Curry Accompaniments (shown on page 91)
Beer or Ale

Curried Clams (Inspired American!)

>   25 small clams, chopped fine
>   2 tablespoons butter
>   1 tablespoon flour
>   ½ cup clam juice
>   ¼ cup cream or sour cream
>   ¼ teaspoon curry powder (more
>   or less as desired)
>   dash Tabasco
>   salt and pepper to taste
>   3 tablespoons sherry
>   ½ teaspoon minced parsley
>   ½ cup salted peanuts or almonds,
>   chopped coarsely.

Behind the Scenes — Prepare clams, or open can and separate juice from minced clams. Mix cream or sour cream with curry powder. Mince parsley; chop nuts. Prepare rice and keep warm.

Before the Guests — Melt butter in chafing dish of blazer pan, directly over flame. Blend in flour and add clam juice. Stir until creamy. Add minced clams and heat well. Add cream or sour cream mixed with curry, season with salt and pepper and a dash of Tabasco. Add chopped nuts. Cook until thoroughly heated. Just before serving add sherry. Serve on mounds of boiled rice with a sprinkle of minced parsley.

Tray-Maid	*Menu*
1) butter	Tiny Cocktail Tomatoes
2) minced clams	Curried Clams
3) clam juice	Rice
4) flour	Green Salad
5) cream mixed with curry	with
6) salt and pepper	Grapefruit Quarters
7) Tabasco	Cream Cheese Currant Jelly
8) sherry	Crackers
9) chopped nuts	Coffee
10) parsley, minced	
11) rice	

An Everyday Curry

1 package spaghetti (8 ounces)
3 tablespoons butter or marga-
    rine
4 tablespoons flour
2 cups milk
1 teaspoon curry powder
1 teaspoon salt
⅛ teaspoon pepper
2 tablespoons drippings
1 pound liverwurst, cubed

Behind the Scenes — Cook spaghetti to "el dente." Drain in colander (ready for dipping later into boiling water for reheating at serving time). Cube liverwurst; sauté in drippings until slightly browned.

Before the Guests — Melt butter or margarine in blazer pan of chafing dish. Blend in flour. Add milk gradually and stir and cook until rich and creamy. Add seasonings. Add cubed liverwurst and heat thoroughly. Lower colander of spaghetti into a pot of boiling water; allow to heat through for just a minute or two; drain. Place in large bowl. Pour sauce from blazer pan over spaghetti and toss gently with a fork. Serves 4.

Tray-Maid	*Menu*
1) butter	Shrimps Roumalade
2) milk	Curry
3) flour	Cottage Cheese
4) curry powder	and
5) salt and pepper	Watercress Salad
6) cubed liverwurst	Fruit Compote
7) spaghetti	Coffee

Oysters with Curry Sauce

1 dozen large oysters
2 tablespoons butter
1 teaspoon curry powder
½ cup oyster liquor
1 teaspoon cornstarch
½ cup cold water

¼ teaspoon salt
minced parsley
toast points
1 can shoestring potatoes (or 1 package quick-frozen)

Behind the Scenes — Strain oysters, saving liquor. Run fingers through the oysters to remove all bits of shells. Remove shoestring potatoes from can or defrost for heating later. Mince the parsley.

Before the Guests — Heat potatoes in lower pan of chafing dish. Set aside to keep warm. Melt butter in blazer pan. Add curry powder and the oyster liquor. Heat to smooth sauce. Mix cornstarch to smoothness with the cold water. Pour into blazer pan. Add salt. Stir to clear rich sauce. Add oysters, simmer until edges curl. Serve on toast points. Sprinkle minced parsley over top. Serve with the shoestring potatoes. Serves 2.

Tray-Maid

1) butter
2) curry powder
3) oyster liquor
4) cornstarch mixed with water
5) salt
6) oysters
7) toast points
8) parsley, minced
9) shoestring potatoes

Menu

Half Grapefruit with Paprika
Oysters with Curry Sauce
on
Toast Points
Shoestring Potatoes
Macaroons
Coffee

[97]

Lobster with Curry Sauce

            2 live lobsters (about 1½ pounds
                each)
            2 tablespoons butter
            1 small onion, minced
            1 tablespoon curry powder
            1 teaspoon salt
               juice of 1 lemon
           ⅛ teaspoon sugar
            1 teaspoon browned flour
            2 cups broth (canned or home-
                made)

Behind the Scenes — Split live lobsters into halves, clean, rinse, and then cut into pieces. Mince onion. Squeeze lemon. Note instructions for browning flour (page 16). Cook rice and keep warm.

Before the Guests — Melt butter in blazer pan of chafing dish; add onion and curry powder. Sauté until onion is soft; add remaining ingredients (except the lobster). Simmer until blended. Add the prepared lobster. Cover; simmer until lobster is cooked through. Baste well before serving. Serves 2 to 4.

Tray-Maid	*Menu*
1) lobsters, cut in serving-size	Melon with Lime
pieces	Lobster with Curry Sauce
2) rice kept warm	Boiled Rice
3) butter	Watercress and Sliced Oranges
4) minced onion	Pastry
5) curry powder	Coffee
6) salt	
7) lemon juice	
8) sugar	
9) browned flour	
10) broth	

Rijsttafel
(Rice Table)

1 large onion, sliced
1 clove garlic
1 tablespoon curry powder
  salt
2 small pieces ginger root
½ cup flour

½ cup drippings
1 cup milk
1 cup chicken broth
2 cups cooked chicken meat
2 cups cooked rice

Behind the Scenes — Prepare rice and keep warm for serving. Slice onion; sliver garlic.   Combine milk and chicken broth. Dice chicken.

Before the Guests — Melt drippings in blazer pan of chafing dish.   Sauté the onion, garlic until soft.   Add salt, curry and ginger.   Simmer for 3 minutes.   Strain and discard onion and spices.   Add flour to strained drippings and blend thoroughly.   Add combined milk and chicken broth gradually, stirring constantly until thickened.   Add chicken and place blazer pan over hot water.   Cover and cook for 8 to 10 minutes to blend flavors.   Serve over a mound of hot rice.

Tray-Maid

1) drippings
2) onion, sliced
3) garlic
4) salt
5) curry powder
6) ginger
7) flour
8) milk and chicken broth combined
9) chicken, diced
10) relish tray
     (See Page 91)

Menu

Rijsttafel
Relish Tray
Fresh Pineapple
Tea

Note: Curry powder is not used in real Rijsttafel but rather a blend of seasonings. However, since it is difficult to get this blend of seasonings in American kitchens, it is necessary to use curry powder.

Japanese Sukiyaki

2 tablespoons beef fat or suet, cut finely
1½ cups onions, sliced thin
½ cup bamboo shoots, sliced thin
1 cup spinach leaves, shredded
1 cup sliced mushrooms
1 pound lean beef, sliced thin
⅛ cup sugar
3 tablespoons shoyu sauce
1 square bean curd, sliced thin
½ cup water
½ cup white wine or saké
2 cups cooked rice

Behind the Scenes — Have the butcher slice the beef very thin (⅛ inch). Slice onions, bamboo shoots, bean curd and mushrooms paper thin. Shred spinach leaves. Chop suet very finely.

Note: This is a stew in which no ingredient should be cooked too long. It has very little gravy, which is never thickened. The proper preparation and attractive decoration of the vegetables is the secret of good Sukiyaki. (However, the original custom, if the dish is being cooked in the family, is for everyone at the table to help stir the dish.)

Before the Guests — Place suet in blazer pan of the chafing dish. Heat and when melted add onions, bamboo shoots, spinach leaves and mushrooms. Simmer for 5 minutes and carefully push to one side of the pan. Add sugar and shoyu sauce, stir to blend; then add meat and fry quickly. Add bean curd and water; simmer about 15 minutes, adding the wine a little at a time as needed to allow the sauce to seep through all ingredients. Arrange the whole attractively on a hot platter and let each one help himself. Serve rice in individual bowls. Serves 4.

Tray-Maid	*Menu*
1) suet, finely chopped	Consommé Julienne
2) onions, sliced	Shrimps Tempava
3) bamboo sprouts, sliced	Sukiyaki
4) spinach leaves, shredded	Individual Rice Bowls
5) mushrooms, sliced	Rice Cake and
6) sugar and shoyu sauce	Japanese Preserved Fruit
7) water	or
8) beef, sliced thinly	Fresh Persimmons or Oranges
9) bean curd, sliced	Tea in Covered Cups
10) wine	
11) rice, kept warm	

Chicken Normandy

2 small broilers
½ cup sweet butter
⅓ cup apple brandy
6 shallots, chopped (or 1 medium-sized onion)
1 tablespoon parsley, minced

1 sprig fresh thyme (or pinch of powdered thyme)
½ teaspoon salt
⅛ teaspoon freshly ground black pepper
6 tablespoons apple cider
6 tablespoons heavy cream

Behind the Scenes — Cut chickens into halves. Measure butter; chop shallots; mince parsley. Measure brandy, apple cider, and cream.

Before the Guests — Melt butter in blazer pan of chafing dish. Sauté chicken pieces, turning to coat pieces well (about ten minutes). Pour apple brandy over and blaze. When flame dies down add shallots, parsley and thyme (if fresh is used, it may be fished out when cooking is finished). Add salt and pepper and apple cider; cover. Continue cooking until chicken pieces are tender and cooked through (about fifteen minutes). Just before serving blend in slowly the cream, rectify seasoning and serve piping hot. Serves 4.

Tray-Maid

1) butter
2) chicken pieces
3) apple brandy
4) shallots
5) parsley
6) thyme
7) salt and pepper
8) apple cider
9) cream

Menu

Avocado Cocktail
Chicken Normandy
Green Peas   Savory Potatoes
Cottage Pudding
with
Bourbon Sauce
Coffee

Scallops Chablis in Patty Shells

½ pound mushrooms, sliced
2 pounds scallops
1 cup water
1 cup Chablis
1½ tablespoons butter
1 medium-sized onion, finely
  chopped
1 tablespoon flour

1 teaspoon minced parsley
dash of cayenne
salt and pepper to taste
4 egg yolks, well beaten
1 cup cream
1 tablespoon butter
2 teaspoons lemon juice
patty shells

Behind the Scenes — Wash and slice mushrooms. Wash scallops and blanch by boiling them for 3 minutes in an equal amount of water and Chablis, barely enough to cover. Drain; reserve liquid. Cut scallops in halves or quarters, if large. Mince onion and parsley. Beat egg yolks and combine with cream. Squeeze lemon. Heat patty shells and keep warm for serving.

Before the Guests — Melt the 1½ tablespoons of butter in blazer pan of chafing dish. Sauté onion until soft; add mushrooms and sauté for 3 minutes. Blend in flour and add 1 cup of the liquid from scallops. Stir constantly over a low flame until sauce is smooth. Add parsley and cayenne and season with salt and pepper. Add scallops and bring mixture to a boil. Gradually add the cream mixed with the egg yolks. Place pan over hot water to prevent boiling and continue to stir until mixture is thickened. Add the 1 tablespoon of butter and lemon juice. Blend well and serve in the heated patty shells. Serves 4 to 6.

Tray-Maid	*Menu*
1) butter	Celery and Carrot Curls
2) minced onion	Scallops Chablis in Patty Shells
3) sliced mushrooms	Minted Green Peas
4) flour	Hot Buttermilk Biscuits
5) liquid in which scallops were blanched	Peach Melba
6) minced parsley	Coffee
7) seasonings	
8) scallops	
9) cream mixed with egg yolks	
10) lemon juice	
11) heated patty shells	

Classic Shrimps

       2 pounds shrimps
      ¼ pound butter
      ½ cup minced onion
      ¼ cup finely minced celery
      ¼ cup finely minced carrot
      ½ cup brandy
     1½ cups white wine (sherry, sau-
           terne, etc.)
      ¼ cup tomato sauce
         an herb bouquet
         salt
         freshly ground pepper
         parsley minced

Behind the Scenes — Shell and clean the raw shrimp; remove the sand line. Mince onion, celery, parsley, and carrot. Make your herb bouquet by combining 2 sprigs of parsley, 1 sprig of marjoram, 2 sprigs of thyme and ½ bay leaf tied in a piece of cheesecloth. Dry herbs may be used if fresh are not available.

Before the Guests — Melt butter in blazer pan of chafing dish. Add the onion, celery and carrot. Cook 2 minutes and add shrimps. Cook gently for 10 minutes. Pour on brandy and blaze. When flame dies down add wine, herb bouquet, tomato sauce and season to taste with salt and pepper. Simmer until shrimps are tender, but not soft (about 10 minutes). Remove the herb bouquet and serve shrimps piping hot with a sprinkle of minced parsley over the top. Serves 4 to 6.

Tray-Maid	*Menu*
1) butter	Stuffed Olives in Bacon Curls
2) minced vegetables	Classic Shrimps
3) shrimp	Rice
4) brandy	Head Lettuce
5) wine	with
6) herb bouquet	Roquefort Dressing
7) tomato sauce	Fruit Cup with Small Cookies
8) salt and pepper	Coffee

Sweetbreads Teresa

2 pair sweetbreads
1 quart water
1 bay leaf
1 carrot, cut up
1 onion, sliced
juice of 1 lemon
4 slices bacon
¼ cup flour
1 medium-sized onion, minced

1 tomato, skinned
2 tablespoons parsley, minced
pinch of thyme
½ teaspoon salt
⅛ teaspoon freshly ground black
pepper
1 cup white wine (sauterne,
Rhine wine, etc.)
toast

Behind the Scenes — Soak sweetbreads in cold water for 20 minutes. Bring water, to which the bay leaf, carrot, sliced onion and lemon juice have been added, to a boil. Plunge in the sweetbreads and cook for 15 minutes. Drain and plunge into cold water (Save the stock for future use). When cool, skin and remove all fat and gristle. Break them up in small pieces the size of a walnut. Do not cut them. Dredge lightly in flour. Cut bacon in shreds with kitchen scissors. Skin tomato and cut in small pieces; mince onion and parsley.

Before the Guests — Fry bacon shred in blazer pan of chafing dish over flame until crisp but not browned. Remove from pan. Sear the dredged sweetbread pieces in hot bacon drippings for 2 minutes over brisk flame. Lower flame and add onion, tomato, parsley, thyme, salt and pepper. Put in the bacon bits and blend. Cook over medium flame for 5 minutes, then add wine and simmer uncovered for 15 minutes. Serve on hot platter garnished with strips of toast. Serves 4.

Tray-Maid	*Menu*
1) bacon, shredded	Asparagus-Beef Consommé
2) sweetbreads, dredged in flour	Sweetbreads Teresa
3) minced onion	French Peas
4) tomato, cut into small pieces	Strawberries in Port Wine
5) minced parsley	Coffee
6) thyme, salt, pepper	
7) wine	
8) toast strips	

Chipped Beef in Wine-Mushroom Sauce

2 tablespoons butter
¼ pound sliced dried beef, shredded
2 tablespoons flour
1 can condensed cream of mushroom soup
½ cup California white wine

½ cup grated American cheese
1 can mushroom stems and pieces (2 ounces)
2 tablespoons chopped parsley
1 tablespoon sherry wine
baked potatoes

Behind the Scenes — Shred beef and plunge into boiling water. Allow to stand 5 minutes. Drain. Combine sauterne with mushroom soup. Drain can of mushroom pieces. Chop parsley. Bake potatoes and keep warm for serving.

Before the Guests — Melt butter in blazer pan of chafing dish. Add shredded beef and sauté for 3 minutes. Blend in flour. Add soup-wine mixture. Cook and stir until mixture boils and is rich and creamy. Add the cheese. Place pan over hot water and stir until cheese is melted. Add mushrooms, parsley and sherry. Season to taste with freshly ground black pepper and salt, if necessary. Serve over steaming hot baked potatoes. Serves 4.

Tray-Maid	*Menu*
1) butter	Chipped Beef in
2) shredded beef	Wine-Mushroom Sauce
3) flour	over
4) soup-wine mixed	Baked Potatoes
5) cheese	Cole Slaw with
6) mushrooms	Sour Cream and Celery Soup
7) parsley, minced	Pineapple Ice Box Cake
8) sherry	Coffee
9) potatoes, kept warm	

Smelts de Luxe

2 dozen small smelts
1 can lobster meat
1 small onion, minced
  cream to moisten
  seasoning
  Worcestershire sauce
  fine crumbs
4 tablespoons butter or margarine
  lemon

Behind the Scenes — Cut heads from smelts, open; remove bones (if desired—some prefer to cook bones in the smelts. They are small and can be eaten). Mince the lobster meat; add the minced onion and sufficient cream to make paste. Season to taste with salt, pepper, Worcestershire sauce. Stuff the smelts with paste and fasten with toothpicks. Sprinkle with crumbs.

Before the Guests — Sauté the smelts in melted butter in the blazer pan of the chafing dish. Serve with lemon juice. Garnish with watercress. Serves 6.

Tray-Maid	*Menu*
1) butter	Smörgåsbord
2) smelt, prepared	Smelts de Luxe
3) lemon	Asparagus with Hollandaise
4) watercress	Orange Chiffon Pie
	Coffee

Eggs Dartmouth
(Poached to Perfection)

1 can tomato soup (10½
   ounces)
1 can chicken broth (10½
   ounces)
½ clove garlic
   bay leaf, crushed
8 eggs
8 thin slices snappy cheese
   whole-wheat toast
   watercress

Behind the Scenes — No mysteries behind the scenes for this gourmet service. Just have cans of soup opened and mixed. Impale garlic on toothpick. Cut cheese into 8 thin finger-length slices.

Before the Guests — In the blazer pan heat soup with garlic and bay leaf. Slip eggs into pan (as many as it will hold); cover and simmer gently (if necessary over hot water) until eggs are poached. Serve on whole-wheat toast, 2 eggs to each service. Cover each egg with strip of cheese and cover cheese with a bit of the tomato sauce. Garnish with watercress. Serves 4.

Tray-Maid	*Menu*
1) soup in blazer pan	Caviar on Toasted Bits
2) garlic and bay leaf	Eggs Darmouth on Toast
3) eggs	Romaine Salad
4) cheese	Wine
5) whole-wheat toast	Petits Fours Coffee
6) watercress	

Oysters Supreme with Anchovies

2 anchovies
2 dozen oysters
½ cup thin cream
1 egg yolk
salt and pepper
dash of grated nutmeg
rye toast
paprika

Behind the Scenes — Strain the oysters; run fingers through them to remove bits of shell. Chop the oysters fine. Cut slices of rye bread into diamond-shaped pieces for toast. Mix egg yolk with cream.

Before the Guests — Mash the anchovies in the blazer pan of the chafing dish. Add oil from the anchovy tin. Heat over flame. Add oysters and stir until heated through. Add cream mixed with the egg yolk. Stir until whole is richly thick. Add salt and pepper to taste and a dash of nutmeg. Have ready a high pile of rye toast, buttered and sprinkled with paprika. Spread with the oysters supreme and serve at once. Serves 4.

Tray-Maid

1) anchovies
2) anchovy oil from tin
3) oysters, chopped
4) cream, mixed with egg yolks
5) seasonings—check ingredients
6) rye toast
7) paprika

Menu

Head Lettuce
with Roquefort Dressing
Oysters Supreme with
Anchovies on Rye Toast
with
Beer or Wine
Green Onions   Carrot Sticks
Liqueur   Coffee

Crabs Creole

4 soft-shelled crabs
4 tablespoons butter
½ clove garlic
1 small onion, minced
1 small sweet pepper, minced
1 cup tomato juice (fresh or canned)
½ cup chicken broth
½ teaspoon celery salt
fresh mint, finely minced

Behind the Scenes — Clean and cut into halves 4 soft-shelled crabs. Impale the garlic on a toothpick. Mince onion and sweet pepper.

Before the Guests — Melt butter in blazer pan of chafing dish. Add garlic and minced onion and pepper. Sauté until onion is soft. Add tomato juice and chicken broth. Add celery salt. Simmer together until blended. Remove garlic. Add crabs; cover; simmer just 7 minutes and serve on toast. Garnish with fresh mint. Serves 2 to 4.

Tray-Maid

1) butter
2) garlic
3) onion, minced
4) pepper, minced
5) tomato juice
6) chicken broth
7) celery salt
8) crabs
9) toast
10) mint, minced

Menu

Spiced Artichoke Hearts
Crabs Creole on Toast
Tomato-Dill Salad
Brandied Peaches
Coffee

Lobster with Mushrooms

2 live lobsters (about 1½ pounds
  each)
4 tablespoons butter
1 tablespoon flour
½ cup hot water
1 tablespoon Mushroom Catsup
  cayenne
¼ cup sherry
⅛ teaspoon thyme
1 dozen small mushrooms
  salt and pepper

Behind the Scenes — Split lobsters into halves; clean and rinse. Cut into serving pieces. Wash mushrooms, leaving stems in place, and cut in halves lengthwise. Prepare and cook rice; keep warm over hot water.

Before the Guests — Melt butter in blazer pan of chafing dish and sauté lobsters until they turn bright red. Add flour to drippings (pushing lobster to one side to permit mixing flour with butter). Add hot water and Mushroom Catsup, cayenne, sherry and thyme. Stir over heat to a blended sauce. Add mushrooms and simmer together until mushrooms are heated through (about 5 to 8 minutes) and seasoned. Serve with saffron rice.

Tray-Maid	*Menu*
1) butter	Hors d'Oeuvres
2) lobsters, halved	Lobster with Mushrooms
3) flour	Saffron Rice
4) hot water	Blancmange
5) Mushroom Catsup	Coffee
6) cayenne	
7) sherry	
8) thyme	
9) mushrooms	
10) saffron rice kept warm	

Chinese Fried Shrimp

½ pound fresh shrimp
½ teaspoon salt
1 teaspoon cornstarch
¼ cup drippings
2 teaspoons sherry
1 cup cooked peas (fresh,
    canned or frozen)
½ teaspoon sugar
1 teaspoon sesame oil
    salt and pepper to taste

Behind the Scenes — Wash uncooked shrimp, remove shells and sand line. Sprinkle with salt and cornstarch and toss until well coated. If fresh peas are used, cook.

Before the Guests — Melt drippings in blazer pan of chafing dish. When sizzling hot add shrimps and toss until lightly browned and very pink, about 3 minutes. Drain. Add sherry, cooked peas, pepper and salt, sugar and sesame oil. Reheat and serve. Serves 2.

Tray-Maid	*Menu*
1) drippings	Egg Roll
2) shrimp	Chinese Fried Shrimp
3) cooked peas	Chinese Fried Noodles
4) sherry	Kumquats
5) sesame oil	Coffee or Tea
6) sugar	
7) salt and pepper	

Noodles Viennese with Tongue

8-ounce package fine noodles,
   cooked
2 tablespoons butter
2 tablespoons poppy seeds
¼ pound almonds, blanched,
   shredded
creamed tongue

Behind the Scenes — Cook noodles in boiling, salted water to "el dente." Drain in colander (ready for dipping later into boiling water for reheating at serving time). Blanch and skin the almonds and cut into long shredded slivers. Prepare 2 cups of cubed, cooked tongue in a rich cream sauce (cream sauce may be made in bottom pan of chafing dish, if desired, adding cubed tongue). Keep hot for serving.

Before the Guests — Melt butter in blazer pan of chafing dish. Add poppy seeds and almonds. Stir until both are delicately toasted. Bring in the noodles at serving time in a large serving bowl. (Have a pot of boiling water ready; lower colander filled with noodles into this; allow to heat through for just a minute or two. Drain.) Pour poppy seeds and almond sauce over noodles and toss (as you would a salad). Serve with the creamed tongue. Serves 6 to 8.

Tray-Maid	*Menu*
1) butter	Noodles Viennese
2) poppy seeds and almonds	with Tongue
3) noodles	Tossed Green Salad
4) creamed tongue kept hot	Fruit Cheese
	Wine Coffee

Scaloppine Madeira

1 pound veal, cut in thin slices
salt, pepper
orégano
flour
1 clove garlic
4 tablespoons butter
1 tablespoon tomato paste
½ cup Madeira (or sherry)
cheese cut in thin slices
cooked spinach seasoned with
nutmeg and sour cream

Behind the Scenes — Choose veal cut from the leg; cut into very thin slices. Place between pieces of waxed paper and beat with a mallet to make paper-thin. Spread garlic paste over meat. Add sprinkling of pepper and orégano, rubbing it into meat. Dust lightly with flour. Mince garlic and then rub to a paste with a teaspoon of salt. Cook 2 pounds (or a package of quick-frozen) spinach. Add sour cream. Season with nutmeg and keep hot for serving time.

Before the Guests — Melt butter in blazer pan of chafing dish and brown meat quickly on both sides. Remove meat to a plate to keep warm. Add tomato paste and Madeira (or sherry). Stir until bubbling. Return meat to sauce; cover whole surface with thin strips of American cheese. Let sauce bubble gently up through the meat to heat the meat and to soften the cheese. Serve over top of the spinach. Serves 4.

Tray-Maid	*Menu*
1) prepared meat	Sauerkraut-Tomato Juice
2) butter	Crackers
3) tomato paste	Scaloppine Madeira
4) Madeira	with Spinach
5) cheese, cut into thin strips	Potato Puffs
6) prepared spinach	Peaches in Burgundy Wine
	Coffee

Sardines à l'Indienne

For patties:
  2 tablespoons butter
  4 eggs, beaten
  ¼ teaspoon salt
  ¼ teaspoon dry mustard
    dash of cayenne
  1 teaspoon chutney
  1 small tin sardines
For crumbing:
  1 egg mixed with
  1 tablespoon water
    bread crumbs
For sautéeing:
  4 tablespoons butter

Behind the Scenes — Scramble the beaten eggs over low heat in butter with salt, mustard, cayenne, chutney, until thick and almost dry. Remove from heat. Mash the sardines and add to egg. Mix well. Cool. Shape into patties. Then dip in bread crumbs, then in the egg mixed with water, and again into crumbs.

Before the Guests — Melt butter in blazer pan of chafing dish. Sauté the patties until golden brown on both sides. Serve with lemon, if desired, and with chutney as a relish. Serves 3 to 4.

Tray-Maid	*Menu*
1) butter	Pineapple Sticks
2) patties ready for sautéeing	Sardines à L'Indienne
3) lemon	with
4) chutney	Cauliflower Vinaigrette
	Cheese and Crackers
	Cream Cake with
	Bittersweet Chips
	Coffee

Escargot Bourguignonne

50 snails
3 cups water
3 cloves garlic
1 carrot minced
1 onion
1 bay leaf
¼ teaspoon thyme
½ lb. butter
 salt and pepper
 parsley

Behind the Scenes — Boil the snails in salted water for 20 minutes and drain. To three cups of water add 1 clove garlic, carrot, onion, thyme and bay leaf. Bring to a boil and simmer 15 minutes. Add snails and cook 15 minutes longer. Drain. Mix butter with chopped parsley and 2 cloves finely minced garlic. Season well with salt and pepper. Remove snails from shells. Rinse shells. Place a little butter mixture in each shell, replace snail and pack with more butter.

Before the Guests — Place snails in blazer pan over high flame. Place lid on tightly and cook until they are bubbling. Serve at once. Serves 4.

Tray-Maid

1) prepared snails

Menu

Consomme Julienne
Escargot Bourguigonne
Chicory-Romaine Salad
with
Sour Cream Dressing
Strawberries in Burgundy

B.Y.O.A.

CHAPTER FIVE

SERVING A CROWD

Sooner or later, this sort of thing comes to every creature. And while handling a crowd is no easier than chinning yourself 235 times, these selections will get you talked about in the right way. They look somewhat involved, but the results should bring you an offer from the Ritz, at least.

Oysters à la Crème

½ cup butter
1 tablespoon salt
2 bay leaves, finely crushed
2 tablespoons cracker crumbs
1 quart light cream
  dash of nutmeg or mace
3 dozen oysters
1 teaspoon quick-cooking tapioca
2 egg yolks
  toast

Behind the Scenes — Drain oysters. Run fingers through to remove any bits of shell. Separate eggs (reserve egg white for some future dish). Crush bay leaves very fine.

Before the Guests — Melt butter in blazer pan of chafing dish. Stir in tapioca. Add cream gradually; then salt, nutmeg, bay leaves, cracker crumbs. Cook for 10 minutes. *Do not boil.* Add beaten egg yolks and cook for 5 minutes. Add oysters and cook until edges curl. Serve on hot buttered toast with a grind of fresh pepper over top. Serves 8.

Tray-Maid	*Menu*
1) butter	Broiled Grapefruit
2) tapioca	Oysters à la Crème
3) cream	Green Salad
4) salt	Cheese Cake
5) nutmeg	Coffee
6) bay leaves	
7) cracker crumbs	
8) egg yolks	
9) oysters	
10) pepper	
11) toast	

Javanese Nasi Goreng
(Shrimp and Ham with Pepper)

1 cup cooked shrimp, fresh or canned
½ pound boiled ham, thinly sliced
1 tablespoon minced green pepper
¼ tablespoon salt
2 tablespoons butter
5 cups cooked rice
cucumbers

Behind the Scenes — Cook shrimps, remove sand line. Cut shrimps into halves. Cut ham into half-inch pieces. Pare cucumbers, cut in thin slices lengthwise. Keep crisp in refrigerator until ready for use. Cook rice and keep warm over hot water.

Before the Guests — Melt butter in blazer pan of chafing dish. Add shrimp, ham, minced green pepper and salt. Cook 15 minutes. Add rice and toss lightly to blend. Serve on individual plates with a garnish of cucumber slices. Serves 10.

Tray-Maid	*Menu*
1) butter	Avocado Canapés
2) prepared shrimp	Nasi Goreng
3) ham, cut in pieces	Persimmon Salad
4) pepper paste	Chocolate Walnut Torte
5) salt	Coffee
6) rice, cooked and kept warm over hot water	
7) cucumber, sliced	

Mussels Louise

8 dozen mussels
liquor from mussels
6 tablespoons butter
6 tablespoons flour
2 cloves garlic, mashed to paste
with 1 teaspoon salt
4 tablespoons parsley, minced
2 tablespoons fresh dill finely
chopped
juice of ½ lemon

Behind the Scenes — Scrub mussels well. Place in large kettle; cover with water. Allow to stand 2 hours. Discard any that float. Drain. Place 1 inch of water in kettle. Add 1 teaspoon salt. Place mussels in kettle; cover; steam 3 minutes, or until shells begin to open. Remove and take meat from shells. Discard the beards, if any. Mash garlic to paste with salt, using flat side of a knife. Mince parsley and chop dill.

Before the Guests — Melt butter in blazer pan of chafing dish. Add garlic paste, dill, parsley, salt and pepper to taste. Sauté 3 minutes. Blend in flour. Add lemon juice, mussel liquor; cook and stir until sauce thickens. Add mussel meat and simmer 3 minutes. Serves 8.

Tray-Maid	*Menu*
1) butter	Consommé Madrilene
2) mussels, prepared for cooking	Mussels Louise
3) mussel liquor	Potato Chips
4) garlic paste	Romaine Salad
5) dill, chopped	Hot Biscuit Fingers
6) parsley, minced	Lemon Sherbet Cookies
7) salt, pepper	Coffee
8) flour	
9) lemon	

Lamb Kidneys with Ham on Toast

1 dozen lamb kidneys
½ pound boiled ham, julienne
½ cup butter or margarine
2 onions, julienne
2 green peppers, julienne
1 cup tomatoes, fresh or canned
2 tablespoons Worcestershire
   sauce
½ teaspoon quick-cooking tapioca

Behind the Scenes — Cut kidneys into halves, then trim carefully all fat and connective tissue. Cover with cold water (to which 1 tablespoon vinegar is added) and let stand ½ hour; then drain. Keep on ice until ready for use. Cut ham, onions and green pepper julienne.

Note: The quick-cooking tapioca is an especially delicate thickening for a sauce and completely simple to add and to cook. Chop the tomatoes very fine, even if canned ones are used.

Before the Guests — Season kidneys with salt and pepper. Melt butter in blazer pan. Add kidneys and sauté until brown. Add ham and brown. Add tomatoes and let settle to bottom of pan. Add Worcestershire and tapioca. Cook gently 3 to 4 minutes. Spread onions and peppers over top. Cover. Simmer 5 to 6 minutes until onions and peppers are soft. Serves 8 to 10.

Tray-Maid	*Menu*
1) butter	Marinated Mushrooms
2) kidneys, prepared for cooking	Lamb Kidney with Ham
3) ham, julienne	Toasted Shredded Wheat Wafers
4) tomatoes	Stuffed Celery
5) Worcestershire	Cherry Pie
6) quick-cooking tapioca	Coffee
7) onions, julienne	
8) peppers, julienne	

Spaghetti Maison

2 pounds spaghetti, cooked
2 tins anchovies
1 bottle capers
1 small can tomato paste
1 quart strained tomatoes
2 onions, finely minced
½ teaspoon orégano
1 clove garlic, finely minced

1 teaspoon salt
dash of Tabasco or pinch of ground red pepper
1 cup American Burgundy
½ cup olive oil
½ cup minced parsley
¼ pound grated Roman or Parmesan cheese

Behind the Scenes — Spaghetti may be cooked ahead of time. It can then be drained and kept warm, or it may be rinsed quickly in boiling water at serving time to reheat. (But do not allow cooked spaghetti to lie in water, since it will become soggy.) Cook tomato paste and tomatoes together for 30 minutes; rub through strainer.

Before the Guests — Place anchovies with their oil, capers, strained cooked tomatoes, onion, orégano, garlic, salt, pepper in blazer pan of chafing dish. Cover and simmer 20 minutes. Add wine and olive oil. Simmer another 10 minutes. Bring in the hot spaghetti in large mixing or serving bowl. Add the cooked sauce, the parsley and half of the grated cheese. Toss and mix well, as if it were a salad. Serve at once with the extra cheese for everyone to help himself. Serves 8 to 10.

Tray-Maid	*Menu*
1) anchovies	Tossed Green Salad
2) capers	Spaghetti Maison
3) cooked tomatoes	Garlic Bread
4) onion, minced	Fruit Cheese
5) orégano	Coffee
6) garlic, minced	
7) salt, pepper	
8) wine	
9) olive oil	
10) parsley, minced	
11) cheese, grated	

Smoked Turkey Carleton

3 cups seasoned chicken broth (turkey broth, if available)
⅓ cup butter
⅓ cup browned flour
1 cup light cream
dash powdered mace

1 pound smoked turkey meat, thinly sliced
8 small flower heads of broccoli, pre-cooked
¼ pound snappy American cheese, grated
3 cups boiled rice (kept hot)

Behind the Scenes — Browned flour makes a sauce of special flavor. To brown: measure 1 cup flour into a heavy frying pan. Stir over low heat until flour is browned. Store and use as needed. But note that browned flour has lost some of its thickening power and makes a more delicate sauce. Parboil the broccoli and drain.

Before the Guests — Melt butter in blazer pan. Add flour, mix, add cream and broth. Stir until sauce is richly thick. Add powdered mace. Next sink the pre-cooked broccoli flowers down into the sauce. Cover with sliced turkey. Blanket turkey with the cheese. Simmer gently until sauce bubbles up through the turkey and cheese begins to melt. Have handy a very sharp knife to cut turkey top into wedge-shaped serving pieces. Serves 8.

Tray-Maid	*Menu*
1) butter	Half Melon with Lime Juice
2) browned flour	Smoked Turkey Carleton
3) chicken broth	Boiled Rice
4) powdered mace	Sliced Tomatoes
5) broccoli, pre-cooked	Hot Rolls
6) sliced turkey	Mints Salted Nuts
7) cheese, grated	Coffee
8) rice, kept hot	

Chinese Duck (or Chicken)

1 duck or chicken, baked or stewed
1 can sliced pineapple (No. 2½ size)
½ cup butter or drippings
1 can mushrooms (8 ounces)

½ cup soya sauce
1 teaspoon crystallized ginger, finely cut
2 cloves garlic
½ teaspoon salt

Behind the Scenes — Use one large or 2 small ducks or a 4-pound roasting chicken. If duck is used, pre-bake in oven. When cool, cut into serving-size pieces. If chicken is used, bake, braise, or stew as desired. Cut into serving-size pieces before or after cooking. Drain pineapple juice from slices. Open can of mushrooms. Cut ginger fine, then mince. Mash the garlic to a pulp with salt (to do this use flat side of knife on bread board).

Before the Guests — Sauté pineapple slices in butter in the blazer pan until brown. Transfer to lower pan of chafing dish and keep hot. Add mushrooms; sauté in blazer pan until brown. Add soya sauce, pineapple juice, ginger, garlic. Cook to rich sauce. Adjust seasoning as needed. Place cooked fowl in this sauce. Heat gently until piping hot. Serve with rice and slices of pineapple. Serves 8 to 10.

Tray-Maid

1) duck or chicken, pre-cooked
2) pineapple slices
3) butter
4) pineapple juice
5) mushrooms, sliced
6) soya sauce
7) ginger
8) garlic mashed to paste with small amount of salt
9) salt
10) rice, kept warm over hot water

Menu

Clear Jellied Soup
with Lime
Chinese Duck
Sautéed Pineapple   Fluffy Rice
Celery and Cucumber Sticks
Radish Roses
Glacé Kumquats
Tea

Chicken à la King De Luxe

3 cups cooked chicken, diced
1 cup celery, diced, parboiled
1 pimiento, cut into strips
½ pound mushrooms
4 tablespoons butter or margarine
2 cups chicken broth

2 tablespoons cornstarch
¼ teaspoon powdered sage and thyme
1 teaspoon minced onion
½ cup whipped cream
1 dozen patty shells

Behind the Scenes — Cut chicken into neat cubes. Dice celery and parboil 5 to 8 minutes until tender. Wash mushrooms; cut stems into thin slices; slice mushroom tops, if desired. Cut one canned pimiento into thin strips. Mince the onion. Mix cornstarch, sage, and thyme. Then blend these to a paste with the water in which celery has been cooked (let this water cool before blending). Whip cream.

Before the Guests — Melt butter in blazer pan and sauté mushrooms. Add chicken broth; when hot, stir in cornstarch mixed to paste in celery water. Add onion. Stir to rich, clear sauce; then add chicken, celery, pimiento. Simmer until sauce bubbles up through chicken and the whole dish is piping hot. Serve in patty shells. Top with whipped cream. Serves 12.

Variations: Note that a rich milk may be substituted for the chicken broth if desired; or half broth, half cream may be used. Stuffed olives, sliced, may be used in place of pimiento. Almonds or pine nuts may be added.

Tray-Maid

1) butter
2) mushrooms, washed and ready
3) chicken broth
4) cornstarch, mixed to paste with sage and thyme
5) onion, minced
6) chicken, diced
7) celery, diced and parboiled
8) pimiento, cut in strips
9) whipped cream
10) patty shells

Menu

Watercress and Orange Salad
Chicken à la King De Luxe
in Patty Shells
Chilled Asparagus
with Mayonnaise
Lemon Sherbet Cookies
Coffee

Shrimp Wriggle

1½ cups onions, sliced
6 tablespoons butter
2 cups stewed tomatoes (fresh or canned)
4 tablespoons cornstarch
4 cups shrimp, cooked
salt
pepper
dash of mace
toast points

Behind the Scenes — Shell and cook shrimp. (Be sure to remove sand line before cooking.) Pare and slice onions. Mix cornstarch with a little cold water to make a liquid paste. Prepare toast points.

Before the Guests — Sauté onions in butter in blazer pan of chafing dish until golden brown. Add tomatoes. Simmer for 10 minutes. Add cornstarch paste; cook and stir until mixture thickens. Add shrimp. Season to taste with salt, pepper and mace. Continue cooking for another ten minutes. Serve piping hot on buttered toast points. Serves 8 to 10.

Tray-Maid	*Menu*
1) butter	Fresh Pineapple Chunks
2) onions, sliced	Shrimp Wriggle
3) tomatoes	Shoestring Potatoes
4) cornstarch paste	Tossed Green Salad
5) shrimp, cooked	Butterscotch Chiffon Tarts
6) seasonings—check ingredients	Coffee
7) toast	

Tuna, the Hawaiian Way

½ pound bacon, sliced
3 cups elbow macaroni, cooked
1 dozen green onions
1 pound mushrooms
½ cup soya sauce
1 pound canned tuna

Behind the Scenes — Cook the macaroni in boiling salted water. Drain. Cut onions, green tops as well as white stalks, into inch-long pieces. Slice mushrooms. Cut bacon into bits.

Before the Guests — Cook the bacon in blazer pan until crisp. Add onion and mushrooms. Sauté until soft (but do not overcook and destroy green of the onions). Add soya sauce and when hot add both cooked macaroni and the tuna. Stir gently with a fork until mixed with sauce. Heat well. Add additional soya sauce, according to taste. Serve in Chinese bowls with boiled rice on side, if desired. Serves 10 to 14.

Tray-Maid	*Menu*
1) bacon, cut in bits	Tossed Green Salad
2) onions, cut	Tuna, The Hawaiian Way
3) mushrooms, sliced	Boiled Rice
4) soya sauce	Watermelon Pickles
5) cooked macaroni	Baked Bananas with Lime Juice
6) tuna	Coffee

Chicken with Chestnuts in Wine Sauce

½ cup butter or margarine
1 onion
3 cups cooked chicken meat
1 zucchini
1 clove garlic
1 tin chicken broth (10½ ounces)
1 teaspoon salt
2 tablespoons Worcestershire sauce
2 dozen chestnuts, shelled and blanched
1 cup blanched almonds
1 cup dry red wine
1 tomato, scalded and skinned
⅛ teaspoon pepper
1 can Chinese fried noodles (12 or 14 ounces)

Behind the Scenes — Cut chicken meat into large cubes. Wash and cut zucchini into cubes. Parboil 5 minutes. Mince onion. Shell and blanch chestnuts. Blanch and skin almonds. Toast chestnuts and almonds in a little butter. Scald and skin a ripe tomato, cut fine. Open can of noodles; heat and keep warm. Cut garlic into halves and impale on toothpicks.

Before the Guests — Melt butter in blazer pan. Add minced onion and garlic; sauté until onion is soft. Add chicken, zucchini, chicken broth, salt, pepper, Worcestershire. Cover; simmer until chicken is heated through and zucchini softened. Add wine and tomato. Cook until blended. Discard garlic. Spread toasted chestnuts and almonds over top. Simmer uncovered until nuts are heated. Serve with hot fried noodles on the side. Serves 12 to 14.

Tray-Maid	*Menu*
1) butter	Melon Balls with White Grapes
2) minced onion	and Cherries
3) garlic	Chicken with Chestnuts
4) chicken, cubed	in Wine Sauce
5) zucchini, parboiled and cubed	Fried Noodles
6) chicken broth	Broccoli Vinaigrette
7) salt and pepper	Apricot Bombe
8) Worcestershire sauce	Coffee
9) wine	
10) tomato, skinned and finely cut	
11) chestnuts and almonds	
12) fried noodles	

Chicken and Broccoli au Vin

3 cups chicken meat cut into cubes
2 packages frozen broccoli
2 tablespoons butter
1 tablespoon lemon juice
  salt and pepper
  10½-ounce can cream of mushroom soup
½ cup heavy cream
½ cup real mayonnaise
½ cup sauterne
½ cup snappy cheese, cut fine
  garlic
  grated Parmesan cheese
  watercress

Behind the Scenes — Thaw the broccoli; open can of soup. Crisp the watercress.

Before the Guests — Rub both the lower pan and the blazer well with cut side of garlic. Place broccoli in lower pan. Cover with chicken. Dot with butter. Sprinkle with salt, pepper and lemon juice. Heat piping hot. Cover and set aside to keep hot. Put soup and cream to heat in blazer pan directly over the flame. When hot add garlic, wine and cheese. Heat gently until cheese melts. Stir in mayonnaise. Remove garlic. Remove chicken from lower pan and immerse in sauce. Cover with broccoli. Heat until sauce bubbles up and over the broccoli. Sprinkle with grated Parmesan. Garnish with watercress. Serves 8 to 10.

Tray-Maid	*Menu*

1) garlic, cut clove
2) broccoli
3) turkey, cubed
4) butter
5) salt and pepper
6) lemon juice
7) mushroom soup
8) cream
9) wine
10) cheese
11) watercress

Sliced Oranges
Turkey and Broccoli Au Vin
Potato Chips
French Bread
Tossed Salad
Cheese
Coffee

Eggs à la King

½ cup butter or margarine
½ pound mushrooms, sliced
½ cup flour
1 quart hot milk
2 teaspoons salt
1 small can pimiento, chopped
8 hard-cooked eggs
½ pound snappy (firm) American cheese
toast triangles

Behind the Scenes — Wash and slice mushrooms. Measure butter, flour, milk. Cook eggs; shell and quarter. Cut cheese in cubes.

Before the Guests — Heat milk in lower pan of chafing dish. Keep warm until needed. Melt butter in blazer pan. Add mushrooms and sauté for 5 minutes. Push mushrooms to one side and add flour. Mix to a smooth paste. Add hot milk; cook and stir until sauce thickens and becomes rich and creamy. Add salt and pimiento. Add the quartered eggs and heat thoroughly. Just before serving add cheese cubes and stir carefully just enough to coat with sauce. Serve on toast triangles. Serves 8.

Tray-Maid	*Menu*
1) milk	Ham Cornucopias
2) butter	Eggs à La King
3) mushrooms, sliced	Hot Potato Chips
4) flour, measured	Vegetables and Mayonnaise Salad
5) salt	Fresh Fruit
6) pimiento, chopped	Coffee
7) eggs, cooked and quartered	
8) cheese, cubed	
9) toast	

Chili Con Carne

1 pound tender round steak, cubed
1 pound lamb, cubed
¼ cup drippings
1 onion, minced
1 teaspoon dried orégano
1 clove garlic
1 teaspoon salt

1 bay leaf, crushed
1 pint tomatoes, fresh or canned
1 cup ripe olives
2 tablespoons chili powder
1 cup hot water
1 pint can kidney beans
  or 1 quart can hominy

Behind the Scenes — Be sure to secure only tender steak and cut it into small cubes. Cut lamb into small neat cubes. To save time when guests are present, cook these together in the drippings in the blazer pan for 15 minutes. They can be reheated later. Mince onion. Stone the olives and mince. Mash the garlic to a pulp with the salt. Have kidney beans open and ready (note that a can of hominy is often substituted for the kidney beans in the Southwest—pleasantly different). Note, too, that chili is often prepared without kidney beans, to be served with frijoles (this is mainly in large cities, where frijoles may be purchased ready to eat).

Before the Guests — Reheat the meat in blazer pan over the flame and add onion. Sauté until onion is tender. Add garlic, bay leaf, very finely crushed, tomatoes, olives, chili powder, water. Cover and cook about 10 minutes, stirring to blend the contents. Adjust the seasoning with salt, pepper and additional chili powder if desired. Add kidney beans. Heat piping hot. Serves 12 generously.

Tray-Maid	*Menu*
1) meat, pre-cooked in blazer pan	Tossed Green Salad
2) onion, minced	Chili Con Carne
3) garlic, mashed to pulp	Fresh Fruit
4) seasonings (check recipe)	Coffee
5) olives	
6) tomatoes	
7) water	
8) kidney beans	

Mexican Peas with Eggs

4 slices bacon, cut fine
4 tablespoons butter
1 small onion, minced
2 cups cooked peas (quick-
    frozen, fresh, or canned)
2 slices whole-wheat bread

2 tablespoons water
8 eggs
¼ cup cheese
½ teaspoon salt
½ teaspoon chili powder
    toast points
    watercress

Behind the Scenes — Cut the bacon into bits, ready for use. Mince the onion. Cook the peas. Soak the bread in water, then press dry and shred into bits. Break eggs into bowl. Add water. Cut cheese to bits.

Before the Guests — Sauté the bacon until crisp. Add butter and onion and continue cooking until onion is soft. Add peas and bread. Heat through. Stir in eggs, cheese, seasonings. Then place pan over hot water and stir until eggs are fluffy and cooked to desired degree. Garnish with watercress. Serve with hot toast points. Serves 8 to 10.

Tray-Maid

1) bacon, minced
2) butter
3) onion, minced
4) bread, moistened and
    shredded
5) peas
6) eggs, slightly beaten with wa-
    ter added
7) cheese, cut fine
8) seasonings
9) watercress
10) bread for toasting

Menu

Chilled Grapefruit with Wine
(poured into center
before serving)
Mexican Peas with Eggs
Frenched String Beans
Vinaigrette
Cinnamon Toast
Brazilian Chocolate
(chocolate and coffee)

B.Y.O.A.

B.Y.O.A.

CHAPTER SIX

LATE SNACKS

The Late Snack is a cherished ritual of American life. It got its glorious start in the days of Diamond Jim Brady, when he was wont to escort Lillian Russell and other buxom beauties into Delmonico's after the theater. There the chafing dishes gleamed and flamed, and enormous dishes were prepared in rapid succession. This happy custom prevails today after bridge, movies, or the theater. Welsh Rabbits and Lobster Newburgs are perhaps top favorites. You will find many other gems in this chapter.

Welsh Rabbit

        2 tablespoons butter
        2 tablespoons flour
        1 cup milk
        ½ teaspoon salt
          dash of pepper
          dash of cayenne
        ½ teaspoon paprika
        ½ cup grated cheese
        2 teaspoons prepared mustard
        1 egg

Behind the Scenes — Very little preparation beforehand. Just set up your tray. Measure milk and cheese.

Before the Guests — Melt butter in blazer pan of chafing dish. Add flour; mix to smoothness. Add milk, salt, pepper, cayenne and paprika. Stir to rich sauce. Place pan over hot water; add cheese. When cheese is melted, add egg mixed with the mustard. Stir until blended. Serve on toast or crackers. Serves 4.
Note: Garlic toast is especially good.

Tray-Maid	*Service Hint*
1) butter	Welsh Rabbit
2) flour	Paprika Celery Curls
3) milk	Garlic Toast
4) salt, pepper	Beer
5) cayenne	
6) paprika	
7) grated cheese	
8) egg mixed with mustard	
9) toast or crackers	

King of Chafing Dishes
(Lobster à la Newburg)

3 lobsters (1½ pounds each)
4 tablespoons butter
½ teaspoon paprika
½ cup sherry or madeira
1½ cups cream
4 egg yolks, well-beaten
1 tablespoon cognac
toast

Behind the Scenes — Cook lobsters in boiling salted water for 20 minutes. Remove meat from shells and cut into ½ inch slices.

Before the Guests — Melt butter in blazer pan of chafing dish. Add lobster meat and sauté it over the direct flame until the outside becomes bright red. Sprinkle with paprika and add wine. Cook until the wine is almost reduced. Place blazer over hot water and add cream mixed with the well-beaten egg yolks. Stir gently until the sauce is thickened. Add cognac. Serve on freshly-made toast.

Tray-Maid	*Menu*
1) butter	Melon Ball Cup
2) lobster meat	Lobster à la Newburg
3) paprika	on Toast
4) wine	Minted Sliced Orange Salad
5) cream mixed with egg yolks	Spice Cake
6) cognac	and
7) bread for toast	Whipped Cream
	Coffee

Cheese Fritters

1 cup cooked rice
1 egg
1 tablespoon milk
½ cup grated snappy cheese (or Swiss cheese)
2 teaspoons prepared mustard
¼ teaspoon salt
¼ teaspoon paprika
½ cup fine dry crumbs
4 tablespoons shortening
4 tablespoons butter or margarine

Behind the Scenes — Cook rice, drain, and cool. Melt 2 teaspoons butter in skillet and add fine dry crumbs. Stir and cook to a golden brown. Combine the rice; egg, slightly beaten; milk; cheese; mustard; salt; paprika and crumbs. Shape into thin patties. Place in refrigerator until ready to use.

Before the Guests — Melt the shortening and butter in blazer pan of chafing dish. Fry the cheese fritters until nicely browned all over and cooked through. Serves 4.

Tray-Maid	*Service Hint*
1) shortening	Cheese Fritters
2) butter	Dill Pickle Slices
3) prepared cheese fritters	Sparkling Cider

Chicken Shortcake

10½-ounce can cream of chicken soup
½ cup light cream
1 cup minced cooked chicken
2 tablespoons parsley, minced
3 tablespoons stuffed olives, chopped

½ teaspoon Worcestershire sauce
2 teaspoons sherry
¼ teaspoon salt
¼ teaspoon paprika
2 tablespoons melted butter
toast rounds
watercress

Behind the Scenes — Combine the chicken soup with the cream. Mix and thoroughly blend rest of ingredients. Set up tray.

For the ambitious hostess — roll out a rich pie dough quite thin. Cut with 3-inch cookie cutter. Place on cookie sheet; prick pastry rounds with fork; cover with second cookie sheet to keep rounds flat during baking. Bake in 400° F. oven 8 to 10 minutes. Use just as you would toast rounds.

Before the Guests — Heat the soup and cream combination in blazer pan of chafing dish. When bubbling stir in the chicken mixture and keep over heat until piping hot. Place a toast round on plate, cover with chicken and top with another toast round, dotting top with just a small amount of chicken. Garnish with watercress. Serves 4 generously.

Tray-Maid

1) chicken soup mixed with cream
2) chicken mixture
3) toast rounds
4) watercress

Service Hint

Chicken Shortcake
Salted Nuts
Cranberry Cocktail

Zesty Kipper Snacks

1 can kipper snacks
2 egg whites
1 tablespoon parsley, minced
1 tablespoon minced chives
3 tablespoons butter
  prepared mustard
  toast triangles

Behind the Scenes — Flake kipper snacks. Place egg whites in bowl and keep at room temperature for beating. Set up tray.

Before the Guests — Beat egg whites until stiff, but still moist. Fold in the flaked snacks, parsley and chives. Melt butter in blazer pan of chafing dish. Spread mixture in pan to form a pancake. Cook slowly over low heat until golden brown. Turn and brown other side. Cut in wedge-shaped pieces, place a dab of mustard on each serving and place on hot buttered toast triangles. Serves 6.

Tray-Maid	*Service Hint*
1) egg whites	Zesty Kipper Snacks
2) flaked kipper snacks	Cucumber Sticks and Olives
3) minced parsley	Beer
4) minced chives	
5) butter	
6) mustard	
7) bread for toast	

Cheese Fondue

1 tablespoon butter
1 cup milk
1 cup fine bread crumbs
2 cups grated cheese
½ teaspoon dry mustard
   dash of cayenne
2 eggs, lightly beaten

Behind the Scenes — No beforehand preparation except to set up tray.

Before the Guests — Melt butter in blazer pan of chafing dish. Add milk, and rest of ingredients except eggs. Stir constantly over low heat until cheese is melted. Just before serving beat in the eggs one at a time. Serve over hot toast or toasted crackers. Or serve in large bowl and let the guests dunk. Serves 4 to 6.

Tray-Maid	*Service Hint*
1) butter	Cheese Fondue
2) milk	Olives and Celery
3) bread crumbs	Hot Rum Punch
4) grated cheese	
5) mustard	
6) cayenne	
7) eggs	
8) toast	

Chicken Gruel

    1 cup cooked chicken, finely
        ground
    ½ cup celery (leaves and stalks)
        finely ground
    ¼ cup fine bread crumbs
    ½ teaspoon onion salt
    4 cups chicken broth

Behind the Scenes — Put chicken and celery through food grinder (an onion, too, if desired, to replace the onion salt). Combine with bread crumbs.

Before the Guests — Place chicken broth in blazer pan of chafing dish. When heated add the chicken mixture. Stir and cook until bubbling. Serve with Melba Toast. Serves four.

Tray-Maid	*Service Hint*

1) chicken broth
2) chicken-celery mixture
3) melba toast

Chicken Gruel
Melba Toast

Kipper Snacks and Scrambled Eggs

                    1 can kipper snacks
                    2 tablespoons butter
                    4 eggs
                    ⅛ teaspoon pepper
                    ⅛ teaspoon paprika
                    2 tablespoons minced parsley
                      pinch of rosemary
                      hot buttered toast

Behind the Scenes — Open kipper snacks and flake into small pieces. Set up tray. Mince parsley.

Before the Guests — Melt butter in blazer pan of chafing dish. Add flaked kipper and sauté for 3 minutes. Add minced parsley and rosemary. Break eggs over mixture and cook and stir until eggs are cooked to your preferred taste. Serve on hot buttered toast with a grind of fresh pepper and a sprinkle of paprika. Serves 4 to 6.

Tray-Maid	*Service Hint*
1) butter	Kipper Snacks and Scrambled
2) kipper snacks, flaked	Eggs
3) minced parsley	Potato Chips
4) rosemary	Sanka Coffee
5) eggs	
6) pepper	
7) paprika	
8) bread for toast	

After-Theater Ham an' Eggs

½ pound boiled ham, cubed
4 hard-cooked eggs
½ teaspoon celery seed
½ teaspoon chili powder
¼ teaspoon paprika
1 can cream soup (10½-ounce size—chicken, celery, mushroom, pea)
1 cup light cream
toasted butterflies or patty shells

Behind the Scenes — Cube ham. Cook eggs, shell and cut into eighths. Combine soup with cream, paprika, celery seed. Prepare butterflies in the following way: remove crusts from slices of bread. Spread both sides lightly with butter. Stuff slices of bread down into muffin tins. Place in oven and bake slowly until golden brown.

Before the Guests — Place combined soup and cream in blazer pan of chafing dish. Add chili powder (if desired). Heat to bubbling. Add ham and hard-cooked eggs. Stir gently to coat with sauce and heat thoroughly. Serve in toasted Butterflies or patty shells. Serves 4 to 6.

Tray-Maid

1) combine soup and cream
2) chili powder
3) ham
4) hard-cooked eggs, cut into eighths
5) toasted butterflies or patty shells

Service Hint

After Theater Ham an' Eggs
Olives and Radish Roses
Sanka Coffee

Sardine Toast

2 tablespoons butter
1 tablespoon flour
3 tablespoons stock
1 teaspoon Kitchen Bouquet
½ teaspoon grated lemon rind
   lemon juice
2 drops essence of cloves
1 wineglass sherry
1 teaspoon grated onion
6 or 8 sardines
   toast

Behind the Scenes — Just set up tray and have sardines chopped and mixed with grated onion, ready for use.

Before the Guests — Melt butter in blazer pan of chafing dish. Blend in flour. Add Kitchen Bouquet or Gravy Secret and stock and stir until smooth. Add grated lemon rind, essence of cloves (or you may use 2 or 3 whole cloves and remove before serving), sherry and lemon juice to taste. Add sardines and stir until thoroughly blended and serve piping hot on toast. Serves 4.

Tray-Maid	*Service Hint*
1) butter	Sardine Toast
2) flour	Raw Carrot Sticks
3) Kitchen Bouquet	Ginger-Lime Cocktail
4) stock	
5) lemon rind and juice	
6) essence of cloves	
7) sherry	
8) sardines, chopped and mixed with onion	
9) toast	

Herring à l'Anglaise

1 Yarmouth bloater with roe
milk
yolks of 2 hard-cooked eggs
1 tablespoon olive oil
1 teaspoon grated onion
1 tablespoon tarragon vinegar
1 teaspoon paprika
toast

Behind the Scenes — Soak fish in milk until soft enough to handle for skinning. Drain; skin and bone. Place in mortar with the egg yolks and pound to a paste. Set up tray.

Before the Guests — Place oil, grated onion, vinegar, paprika in blazer pan of chafing dish. Blend and add paste. Stir constantly until well mixed and hot. Serve on toast. Serves 4 to 6.

Tray-Maid	*Service Hint*
1) olive oil	Herring à L'Anglaise
2) grated onion	Pickle Relish
3) vinegar	Mulled Cider
4) paprika	
5) fish paste	
6) bread for toast	

B.Y.O.A.

B.Y.O.A.

CHAPTER SEVEN

QUICK AND EASY

These delicious, rapid repasts are just the ticket for languid
Sunday evenings, or for the dark days following quarterly
income-tax disbursements. These savory compounds will
still that distant drum which pounds inside your skull. One
calls for a *special* scream from the eagle—Oysters Creamed
American!

Oysters Creamed American

2 dozen oysters shucked
4 tablespoons butter
6 tablespoons flour
½ teaspoon salt
⅛ teaspoon pepper
3 tablespoons parsley minced
1 cup heavy cream
1 cup rich milk
1 pimiento, diced
pinch cayenne
3 tablespoons sherry wine
buttered toast

Behind the Scenes — Run fingers through oysters to remove any bits of shell. Strain oyster liquor through a cloth to remove any sand. Cut oysters with scissors into pieces. Mince parsley; dice pimiento.

Before the Guests — In lower pan of chafing dish heat oysters in their own liquor for 3 minutes, or until edges curl. Melt butter in blazer pan over medium flame. Blend in flour; gradually add cream and milk combined, stirring constantly. Then add oyster liquor, stir vigorously until sauce is smooth, rich and creamy. Simmer gently for 3 minutes, stirring constantly. Add pimiento, cayenne, salt, pepper and oysters. Heat to piping hot. Add sherry wine, blend well and serve immediately on hot buttered toast. Garnish with sprinkle of parsley.

Tray-Maid

1) oysters and oyster liquor
2) butter
3) flour
4) cream and milk combined
5) pimiento, diced
6) seasonings, check ingredients
7) sherry
8) parsley, minced
9) toast

Service note: Nothing tops this dish for a Sunday night meal. A cup of broth to begin with, a tart green salad, a wedge of cheese— and what more could any one ask for?

Midnight Eggs

2 tablespoons butter
3½-ounce can mushrooms
  (chopped)
6 to 8 eggs
¼ teaspoon salt
  dash of pepper
1 tablespoon water
  toasted English muffins

Behind the Scenes — Chop mushrooms if necessary (or slice if you wish). Set up tray.

Before the Guests — Melt butter in blazer pan of chafing dish, directly over flame. Add mushrooms and sauté until delicately browned. Place blazer pan over hot water and add the eggs, one after the other, stirring quickly with a swirling motion as they slide into the steaming butter. Add salt, pepper and water. Stir steadily until eggs are high and handsome. Serve on toasted English muffins.

Tray-Maid

1) butter
2) mushrooms
3) eggs
4) salt and pepper
5) water
6) English muffins

Service note. Variety is the spice of life—if you wish to make changes add:

1. A drift of grated cheese over top of eggs (try grated Swiss)
2. A dollop of strawberry preserve with a crest of sour cream over each serving
3. Spread the muffins with anchovy paste, snappy cheese or Virginia ham spread
4. Sprinkle top of eggs with paprika or just a whiff of chili powder
5. Instead of muffins use day-old bread sautéed in garlic butter or just plain butter
6. Remove tops from hot popovers and fill with eggs
7. Use tomato juice or sherry wine instead of water

[151]

Asparagus-Corn Rabbit

1 can condensed cream of
    asparagus soup
1 cup cream style corn
½ pound grated cheddar cheese
½ teaspoon mustard
½ teaspoon Worcestershire sauce
    dash of cayenne
2 eggs, beaten until light and
    foamy
    hot toast
    paprika

Behind the Scenes — Very little preparation needed for this dish other than to grate the cheese and open tins of soup and corn.

Before the Guests — Combine asparagus soup and corn in blazer pan of chafing dish. Place over hot water and heat. Add cheese, mustard, Worcestershire sauce and a dash of cayenne. Cook and stir until cheese is melted. Remove and add a little of the mixture to the beaten eggs; then add eggs to whole mixture, folding in lightly. Return to heat and cook until blended and heated thoroughly. Serve on hot toast with a garnish of paprika.

Tray-Maid

1) asparagus soup
2) corn
3) grated cheese
4) mustard
5) Worcestershire sauce
6) cayenne
7) eggs
8) toast
9) paprika

Service note: This provides a wonderful combination of flavors. For variety you may want to try—

Tomato Rabbit: Place 1 can condensed tomato soup in blazer pan over hot water. When heated add 1 cup grated American cheese, stirring constantly until cheese is melted. Add milk and remove from heat. Add mustard to beaten egg and add to cheese mixture. Blend well, return to heat and cook, stirring constantly until piping hot. Serve on toast.

Easy Shrimp Creole

¼ cup finely-chopped celery
1 medium-sized onion, chopped
3 tablespoons salad oil
½ cup water
1 can condensed tomato soup
    (10½ ounces)
1 teaspoon wine vinegar
2 (5-ounce) cans shrimp or 2
    cups cooked shrimp (fresh
    or frozen)
2½ cups cooked rice (leftover
    rice may be used)

Behind the Scenes — Chop celery and onion. If fresh or frozen shrimp are used, remove sand line. Cook rice; keep warm over hot water. (If leftover rice is used, heat over hot water.)

Before the Guests — Cook celery and onion in salad oil in blazer pan of chafing dish until tender. Blend in water, soup and vinegar. Simmer 10 minutes; add shrimp and heat thoroughly. Serve over a mound of hot fluffy rice.

Tray-Maid

1) chopped celery and onion
2) salad oil
3) water
4) tomato soup
5) vinegar
6) shrimp
7) rice (kept warm over hot
    water)

Service note: Here is a wholesome, flavorful dish to help stretch that food dollar, made and served steaming hot right at the table. Vary the flavor with herbs —a pinch of rosemary or thyme, basil or orégano.

Tiny Corn Fritters

1 can whole kernel corn
1 tablespoon heavy cream
1 tablespoon grated onion
½ teaspoon salt
⅛ teaspoon freshly-ground black
    pepper
4 eggs
2 tablespoons butter

Behind the Scenes — Drain can of corn. Combine with well-beaten eggs, onion, cream, salt and pepper.

Before the Guests — Melt butter in blazer pan of chafing dish. When sizzling, drop mixture by teaspoonfuls and brown all over. (They should be no larger in size than an oyster.)

Tray-Maid

1) butter
2) corn mixture

Service note: Make plenty of these, for they are highly popular, whether served alone or with such dishes as delicatessen meats. Especially good as an hors d'oeuvre, impaled on toothpick.

Tomato Fritters

8 medium-sized tomatoes
4 eggs
3 tablespoons bacon drippings
½ teaspoon salt
⅛ teaspoon pepper
¼ cup cracker crumbs

Behind the Scenes — Skin tomatoes and cook until pieces are well broken up. Cool. Beat eggs thoroughly, add tomatoes with the bacon drippings, salt and pepper. Add enough cracker crumbs to make a fairly stiff batter.

Before the Guests — Melt some extra drippings in blazer pan of chafing dish. When sizzling hot, drop tomato batter by spoonfuls and brown on both sides. Serve piping hot.

Tray-Maid

1) drippings
2) tomato batter

Service note: With their high egg content, tomato fritters may be the main dish. They are particularly good with a vegetable plate menu.

Cabbage in a Chafing Dish

1 small head young green cabbage
1 small onion, minced
2 teaspoons caraway seeds
¼ teaspoon salt
⅛ teaspoon pepper
4 tablespoons butter or margarine

Behind the Scenes — Wash cabbage thoroughly and cover with cold water for 20 minutes to crisp. Drain. Shred very fine. Mince onion.

Before the Guests — Melt butter in blazer pan of chafing dish. Sauté onion for 5 minutes; do not brown. Add shredded cabbage (just as much as pan will hold), sprinkle caraway seed over top of cabbage. Cover pan. Cook over flame 5 to 8 minutes, stirring occasionally, or until cabbage is tender. Do not overcook. Season with salt and freshly-ground pepper.

Tray-Maid

1) butter
2) onion, minced
3) cabbage, shredded
4) caraway seed
5) salt and pepper

Service note: Quick, easy and simple but delightfully tasty served with hot or cold slices of tongue or corned beef, a good relish, crusty rolls and a beverage.

Bananas Newburg

4 red bananas, sliced in half
    lengthwise
2 tablespoons butter
2 tablespoons brown sugar
½ cup sherry
¼ cup grated cheese

Behind the Scenes — Peel and slice bananas. Grate cheese. Set up tray.

Before the Guests — Melt butter in blazer pan of chafing dish. Sauté banana halves until tender and brown. Sprinkle brown sugar over top of bananas and pour sherry over them. Simmer a few minutes. Sprinkle generously with the grated cheese and serve hot.

Tray-Maid

1) butter
2) bananas
3) brown sugar
4) sherry
5) grated cheese

Service note: Minus the cheese this would make a good dessert for a soup and salad menu. But with the cheese it is another good main dish for a vegetable plate menu.

Minced Clams in Cream Cheese Sauce

1 package cream cheese (3
  ounce)
1½ cups minced clams (fresh or
  canned)
½ teaspoon garlic salt
¼ teaspoon mustard
1 tablespoon Worcestershire
  sauce

Behind the Scenes — If fresh clams are used you can purchase them shucked (same as oysters). Drain liquid and mince. (There should be at least ½ cup clam liquid.)

Before the Guests — Melt cream cheese with the clam liquor in blazer pan of chafing dish over hot water. Stir to blend well. Add garlic salt, mustard and Worcestershire. Add minced clams and bring to a boil. (If sauce seems too thick add a little fresh or diluted evaporated milk to give it the right consistency.) Serve on hot buttered toast or crisp crackers.

Tray-Maid

1) cream cheese
2) clam liquor
3) garlic salt
4) mustard
5) Worcestershire
6) minced clams
7) hot buttered toast

Service note: This is an excellent luncheon dish. It is also a good canapé to serve with drinks. Crabmeat, oysters, salmon, shrimp or tuna fish may all be cooked and served in this manner.

Heavenly Salmon Hash

1 medium sized onion
2 tablespoons butter
1½ cups cooked sweet potatoes, diced
¼ teaspoon mace
½ teaspoon salt
⅛ teaspoon fresh ground pepper
2 cups canned salmon (1 pound tin)
6 eggs

Behind the Scenes — Your emergency shelf comes into play with this dish to do away with any beforehand preparation. Simply open a can of sweet potatoes and dice. Open salmon tin and flake. Mince onion and set up your tray.

Before the Guests — Melt butter in blazer pan of chafing dish. Sauté onion until tender but not browned. Add potatoes and flaked salmon. Season with salt, pepper and mace. Mix lightly and spread evenly in pan. Cover and cook for 10 minutes over flame. Uncover and make six little hollows. Into each of these hollows break an egg. Season, set cover in place, and cook until eggs are set (about 10 minutes). Serves 6.

Tray-Maid

1) butter
2) onion, minced
3) potatoes, diced
4) salmon, flaked
5) salt, pepper and mace
6) eggs

Service note: Wonderful for a Club-Day Dinner. Serve vegetable salad bowl first. Finish with sherbet or ice and a beverage.

Sweet Potato-Pecan Balls

    2 cups sweet potato pulp
    1 egg
      salt to taste
    2 tablespoons melted butter or
        margarine
    ⅛ teaspoon cinnamon
    1 tablespoon brown sugar
    1 cup pecans crushed

Behind the Scenes — If fresh potatoes are used, cook in jackets, drain and mash. If canned, drain and mash. Combine with slightly beaten egg, butter, cinnamon, brown sugar and salt. Form into balls and roll in crushed pecans.

Before the Guests — Melt butter or margarine in blazer pan of chafing dish and when sizzling hot toss in the potato balls and sauté, tossing to brown all sides, until thoroughly heated and golden brown.

Tray-Maid

1) prepared potato balls
2) butter or margarine for
     sautéeing.

Service note: Leftover white mashed potatoes may be prepared in the same manner. Omit brown sugar, cinnamon. Substitute poppy seeds and roll in crushed walnuts. This is an especially popular Sunday night supper dish when you have leftover cold roast or a cold roast chicken to serve with it.

Asparagus with Cream Sauce

2 pounds fresh asparagus (quick-
   frozen may be used)
1 tablespoon butter
1 tablespoon flour
1 cup light cream
  salt and pepper
  paprika
  toast

Behind the Scenes — Pre-cook asparagus. Keep warm in lower pan of chafing dish.

Before the Guests — Melt butter in blazer pan of chafing dish. Blend in flour. Add cream gradually and season to taste with salt and pepper. Cook and stir until sauce is smooth, rich and creamy. Place a bunch of the drained asparagus on hot buttered toast and top with sauce. Sprinkle with paprika and serve piping hot.

Tray-Maid

1) butter
2) cream
3) salt and pepper
4) paprika
5) asparagus
6) bread for toast

Service note: Feature this on a vegetable luncheon with devilled eggs and tomato salad. A cup of hot chocolate could be both sweet and beverage. Or serve as an individual vegetable with main entrée; omit toast and lay a strip of pimiento across top of sauce for color.

Luncheon Corn

2 cups canned whole kernel corn
   (or 2 cups corn scraped
   from cob)
½ pint light cream
2 tablespoons butter or margarine
2 tablespoons flour
½ teaspoon salt
⅛ teaspoon freshly-ground pepper
½ pound cheese, sliced (American, Cheddar, etc.)
   toast
1 teaspoon caraway seeds

Behind the Scenes — Very little beforehand preparation. Scrape kernels from ears of corn or use the canned corn. Slice cheese.

Before the Guests — Melt butter in blazer pan of chafing dish. Blend in flour. Place pan over water and gradually add cream, stirring constantly until sauce is rich and smooth. Season to taste with salt and pepper. Add corn and continue to cook for 5 minutes, or until mixture is piping hot. Place slices of cheese over top and cover pan. Heat slowly until cheese just begins to melt. Serve at once on thin slices of buttered toast. A few caraway seeds sprinkled on top of each serving make a flavorsome addition.

Tray-Maid

1) corn
2) cream
3) butter
4) flour
5) seasonings
6) cheese
7) toast
8) caraway

Service note: A dish with a flair that will create a fine taste sensation. Add a salad or a bowl of fresh fruit and a beverage and rest on your laurels.

Minced Collops au Naturel

1 pound ground round steak
1 small onion, minced finely
salt and pepper to taste
1 teaspoon brown seasoning
1 tablespoon butter
1 teaspoon Mushroom Catsup
1 tablespoon flour
water

Behind the Scenes — No beforehand preparation for this tasty filling for hot sandwiches. Just set up tray.

Before the Guests — Place the finely-chopped round steak in blazer pan of chafing dish and sauté it in its own juice for about 10 minutes, stirring constantly. Then add butter, onion, pepper, salt, and any of the brown seasonings, such as Kitchen Bouquet, Gravy Secret, Mushroom Catsup and the flour made into a smooth paste with a little extra butter. Add 2 or 3 tablespoons of water to make a smooth sauce.

Tray-Maid

1) beef
2) onion, minced
3) salt, pepper
4) Kitchen Bouquet, Mushroom Catsup or Gravy Secret, etc.
5) butter
6) flour
7) water

Service note: This makes a wonderful hot sandwich (to be served with a fork) the meat forming little kernels as it cooks. It is tasty and good-flavored. Serve between buttered slices of whole-wheat or rye bread with celery curls and radish roses as crunchy greens.

Pepper Beef

    2 green peppers
    1 potato, medium size
    2 stalks celery
    1 large onion
    ½ cup boiling water
    ½ teaspoon Meat Glaze
    2 tablespoons butter, margarine,
        or drippings
        12-ounce can roast beef
        salt and pepper
        paprika

Behind the Scenes — Turn roast beef from can carefully, so as to hold the shape of the mold. Cut the peppers in half lengthwise. Remove seeds and stems. Then cut into long julienne pieces. Scrub potato well—do not pare. Slice very thin, then cut into julienne pieces. Cut celery stalks "on the bias" to get long, thin slivers. Cut onions into julienne pieces lengthwise.

Before the Guests — Place water in blazer pan of chafing dish and when boiling add vegetables and cook for 4 minutes. Add remaining ingredients, placing the mold of canned beef in center of pan. Spread paprika generously over the top of meat. Cover and continue cooking for another 15 or 20 minutes. Serve piping hot.

Tray-Maid

1) water
2) vegetables, julienne
3) Meat Glaze
4) beef
5) butter
6) paprika, salt and pepper

Service note: A quick and easy way of using up odds and ends of vegetables, with the help of the emergency shelf. A meal in a dish.

Ham and a Wonderful Sauce

1 slice smoked ham, ½ inch
  thick
¼ glass currant jelly
2 tablespoons prepared mustard
2 tablespoons grated onion

Behind the Scenes — Just set up the tray.

Before the Guests — Broil the ham slice, whole or cut into serving-size pieces, in blazer pan over the flame. When cooked through (it takes about 20 minutes) remove to platter. Stir jelly, mustard and grated onion into the blazer pan; heat and pour over the ham.

Tray-Maid

1) ham slice
2) currant jelly
3) prepared mustard
4) grated onion

Service note: An elegant dish to build your menu around, and one which will fit any occasion. Just right for that evening at home and super for serving last-minute guests.

Breaded Chicken Slices

1 can luncheon chicken
1 egg, slightly beaten with 1
    tablespoon water
½ cup fine dry bread crumbs
3 tablespoons butter
    minced parsley

Behind the Scenes — Remove chicken from tin, being careful to hold its solid shape. Cut into fairly thick slices. Mix egg with water. Dip chicken slices into breadcrumbs, egg, and again into crumbs.

Before the Guests — Melt butter in blazer pan of chafing dish. When sizzling, place the breaded slices in pan and sauté to a delightful brown on both sides. Serve with a garnish of minced parsley.

Tray-Maid

1) breaded chicken slices
2) butter
3) minced parsley

Service note: This is really a kind of quick and easy croquette. To serve it with a quick and easy sauce, just open a can of cream of mushroom soup. Dilute very lightly with cream (add a touch of curry powder, if desired).

French Toasted Cheese Sandwiches

          3 eggs
          1 cup milk
          ½ teaspoon salt
            dash of cayenne
            bread slices (a day old)
            butter
            American or Cheddar cheese
              (1 slice for every 2 slices of
              bread)

Behind the Scenes — Mix eggs, milk, salt and dash of cayenne. Prepare the sandwiches, ready for toasting: butter the bread, then put together with slices of cheese.

Before the Guests — Melt butter in blazer pan of chafing dish. Dip sandwiches in the egg-milk mixture and sauté in butter until golden brown on both sides and cheese is beginning to melt.

Tray-Maid

1) butter
2) egg-milk mixture
3) prepared sandwiches

Service note: For that midnight snack or busy day lunch. A sweet and a beverage make the meal complete.

Eggs with Tomatoes

8 slices bacon
6 eggs
2 medium-sized tomatoes,
    skinned, cut into small pieces
salt and pepper
paprika
watercress

Behind the Scenes — Skin and cut tomatoes into pieces. Set up tray.

Before the Guests — Try out the bacon in the blazer pan of the chafing dish until delicately *crisp*. Remove to paper towel but keep warm. Add tomatoes to the fat. Simmer until reduced to rich paste. Add salt and pepper to taste. Add eggs, one at a time, stirring as they slide into the tomato gravy. Then place blazer pan over hot water and continue stirring until eggs are cooked to desired degree. Serve with sprinkle of paprika, 2 slices of bacon to each serving with a garnish of watercress on toast points. Serves 4.

Tray-Maid

1) bacon
2) tomatoes, cut into small pieces
3) salt and pepper
4) eggs
5) paprika
6) watercress

Service note: For Sunday morning brunch or Sunday evening supper. This is an appetizing egg dish. Serve with a green salad and top off with fresh fruit and cheese.

Ham and Cheese Puff

4 tablespoons butter
½ pound thinly sliced boiled ham
　　(or ham sausage)
½ pound snappy cheese
　　prepared mustard
2 tablespoons Worcestershire
　　sauce
2 tablespoons snappy French
　　dressing
1 teaspoon caraway seed
2 eggs
2 tablespoons toasted buttered
　　crumbs (optional)
　　black olives

Behind the Scenes — Slice the cheese fairly thin and spread with prepared mustard. Mix Worcestershire, French dressing, caraway seed and eggs. Add dash of salt and pepper, if desired.

Before the Guests — Melt the butter in the blazer pan and brown all the ham, quickly. Remove all but sufficient to cover bottom of pan. Add a layer of sliced cheese, a layer of ham and continue until all are used, with top layer of cheese. Heat gently until cheese is puffing. Beat up the egg mixture (use a fork); pour over top of cheese. Cover and cook just long enough to set the eggs (do not let them dry out). Cover with toasted crumbs, if desired, and sliced black olives. Add a dash of paprika, if desired.

Tray-Maid

1) butter
2) ham
3) cheese, sliced
4) eggs, mixed with Worcester-
　　shire, etc.
5) toasted crumbs
6) black olives, sliced

Service note: This is a sturdy, filling dish. Start off with clear soup; you can heat it in the same chafing dish, and then, while the "Puff" is cooking, enjoy the soup.

Codfish with a New Twist

½ pint light cream
1 cup mashed potatoes
1 cup shredded codfish (the
    packaged type saves soak-
    ing time)
1 onion minced finely
2 tablespoons butter
    fresh ground black pepper

Behind the Scenes — Prepare potatoes. Shred codfish. Set up tray.

Before the Guests — Melt butter in blazer pan of chafing dish. Sauté onion until light golden color. Pour in cream. Heat for 5 minutes. Add the mashed potatoes and shredded fish. Cover and cook slowly until thoroughly heated. Serve piping hot with a generous grind of black pepper on top.

Tray-Maid

1) butter
2) minced onion
3) cream
4) mashed potatoes
5) shredded codfish
6) pepper

Service note: Serve as is for a quick snack; or, if you prefer, it can be browned as you would do hashed browned potatoes. Also, serve as a main dish by making indentations in top and breaking an egg in each hollow. Cover and serve when eggs are poached to preferred degree. A salad and beverage complete a good luncheon.

Golden Buck

1 egg
1 pound mild cheese
½ cup milk
2 tablespoons butter
½ teaspoon mustard
⅛ teaspoon ginger

Behind the Scenes — Break cheese into small pieces, or this may be done right at the chafing dish. Set up tray.

Before the Guests — Melt butter in blazer pan of chafing dish. Place over water. Add half the cheese, broken into small pieces. When melted, add remaining cheese. Melt. Then add slightly beaten egg and milk, stirring constantly. Season and serve immediately on toast or toasted crackers.

Tray-Maid

1) butter
2) cheese
3) egg
4) milk
5) mustard
6) ginger
7) toast or toasted crackers

Service note for the adventurous-minded. Try:

Celery Rabbit: 1 can condensed cream of celery soup placed in blazer pan over hot water. Add ¾ cup grated cheddar; stir until melted. Add ½ cup milk. Then add ¼ teaspoon mustard, ½ teaspoon Worcestershire sauce, ¼ teaspoon paprika to 2 eggs and beat. Add egg mixture to cheese mixture, stirring constantly until well blended and piping hot. Fold in ½ cup cracker crumbs and serve on hot toast. Garnish with ripe olives.

Lobster Lumps Maryland

    1 can lobster (1 pound size)
    4 tablespoons butter
    2 tablespoons flour
    1 cup light cream
    ½ teaspoon salt
    ½ teaspoon paprika
      pinch of cayenne
    1 cup cooked peas, (fresh, fro-
      zen or canned)
    ½ cup sherry
    2 egg yolks, beaten

Behind the Scenes — Open tin of lobster, remove any cartilage and break into fairly large lumps. Separate eggs. Combine flour, salt, paprika and cayenne.

Before the Guests — Melt butter in blazer pan of chafing dish. Blend in seasoned flour. Gradually add cream and cook and stir until sauce thickens and is rich and creamy smooth. Gently fold in the peas and lobster lumps and simmer for 5 minutes. While dish simmers mix egg yolks with the sherry in a measuring cup. Remove pan from flame and stir in the sherry-egg mixture and serve immediately on hot buttered toast points.

Tray-Maid

1) lobster meat
2) butter
3) seasoned flour
4) cream
5) egg yolks
6) sherry
7) peas
8) bread for toast points

Service note: Just right for that gay, festive mood. Fits right in with the party spirit. Draw on the pantry shelf for extras to make the meal a gala affair.

Tongue Burgundy

1 can or jar of tongue (12 ounces)
4 tablespoons butter
4 tablespoons flour
1 cup stock (canned may be used
1 can tomato sauce (8-ounce)
1 can white potatoes (small size)

1 can onions (small size)
½ teaspoon prepared horseradish
¼ teaspoon prepared mustard
½ teaspoon salt
⅛ teaspoon pepper
½ cup American wine (Burgundy, claret, etc.)

Behind the Scenes — Just reach up and take the makings for this dish from your pantry shelf.

Before the Guests — Melt butter in blazer pan of chafing dish. Add any of the meat jelly that clings to the tongue. Blend in flour. Gradually add stock and tomato sauce. Cook and stir until sauce thickens and is rich and smooth. Add horseradish, mustard, salt and pepper to taste. Blend thoroughly. Lay overlapping slices of tongue on sauce in center of pan. Surround with small potatoes and onions. Then pour in wine. Cover and cook until sauce bubbles up over meat and vegetables.

Tray-Maid

1) butter
2) flour
3) stock
4) tomato sauce
5) horseradish
6) mustard
7) salt and pepper
8) tongue, sliced
9) potatoes (leftover boiled or canned)
10) onions
11) wine

Service note: A hearty, filling dish, without leaving the house. Leftover potatoes, or any other leftover vegetables, such as carrots, peas, green or lima beans, celery, may be added. Be sure to give the vegetables character by cutting the carrots and green beans julienne and arranging them in a pattern in the pan.

Kedgeree

2 teaspoons minced onion
1 tablespoon butter
1 teaspoon flour
½ cup light cream
1 tablespoon chopped parsley
4 hard-cooked eggs, chopped
2 cups cooked fish, flaked
½ teaspoon curry powder
2 cups cooked rice
salt and pepper to taste

Behind the Scenes — Cook and flake fish. Cook rice (or left-over fish and rice may be used in this dish). Hard cook eggs and chop coarsely. Mince onion and parsley.

Before the Guests — Place blazer pan over hot water and melt butter. Sauté onion until soft. Blend in flour. Add cream and stir and cook for 5 minutes. Add parsley and chopped eggs. Simmer for 3 or 4 minutes, then add flaked fish, curry, salt, pepper and rice. Toss lightly with a fork. Heat thoroughly. Serve in mounds on hot plates, garnished with extra chopped egg yolk.

Tray-Maid

1) butter
2) onion
3) flour
4) cream
5) parsley
6) chopped eggs
7) fish, flaked
8) curry powder
9) salt and pepper
10) cooked rice

Service note: The New England way of serving this dish is with fried tomatoes for breakfast. In the Far East they cook kedgeree this way: mix ½ pound cold, boiled fish with 1 cup boiled rice, seasoned with salt and pepper. Heat in melted butter. Add 2 cooked egg whites, diced. Turn into serving dish; press cooked egg yolk through a sieve over top. Either way will bring pleasurable eating to your table.

B.Y.O.A.

B.Y.O.A.

CHAPTER EIGHT

SHOW-OFF

This chapter touches something admirable in the human soul.
Who would deny that it is glorious to master these spectacular
dishes, to posture beside flaming brandy? Vain? Perhaps—
but *we* could never resist it!

Eggs Bourguignonne au Champignon

½ pound mushrooms, sliced
2 tablespoons butter or margarine
1 cup Burgundy wine
1 bay leaf
⅛ teaspoon garlic salt

¼ teaspoon dry mustard
⅛ teaspoon nutmeg
2 teaspoons cornstarch
2 teaspoons Kitchen Bouquet
4 eggs
4 slices toast

Behind the Scenes — Wash and stem mushrooms. Chop stems and slice the mushrooms, if small use whole. Mix cornstarch and Kitchen Bouquet together, making a smooth paste.

Before the Guests — Melt butter in blazer pan of chafing dish. Sauté mushrooms about 5 minutes, browning slightly. Remove from pan. Add wine to blazer pan with the bay leaf and garlic salt. Simmer for five minutes. Remove bay leaf. Poach two eggs one at a time in this wine sauce to desired degree. Remove eggs to hot toast on individual serving dishes; keep warm. Add the cornstarch paste to wine with the mustard and nutmeg. Add mushrooms and cook and stir gently for 5 to 10 minutes or until cornstarch is thoroughly cooked. Arrange wine-mushroom sauce over eggs, then a generous grind of fresh pepper. Serve immediately. Serves 4.

Tray-Maid

1) butter
2) wine
3) bay leaf
4) garlic salt
5) mushrooms, cooked
6) eggs
7) hot toast
8) cornstarch paste
9) mustard
10) nutmeg
11) pepper

Menu

Stuffed Celery
Eggs Bourguignonne
au Champignon
Shoestring Potatoes
Broiled Tomato
Hearts of Lettuce with
Thousand Island Dressing
Zabaglione
Coffee

Sweetbread and Mushroom Ragoût

> 1 pair sweetbreads
> 1 can mushrooms (4 ounces)
> 3 tablespoons butter
> 1 tablespoon cornstarch
> 1 can chicken broth (10½-
>   ounce tin)
>   dash of powdered sage and
>   rosemary
> ¼ cup shredded coconut

Behind the Scenes — Parboil sweetbreads about 10 minutes, then plunge into cold water. Remove membrane and tubes. Cut into cubes. Open tin of mushrooms. Mix cornstarch with the broth, adding water and mushroom liquor to make 1 (measuring) cup (½ pint). Add sage and rosemary to broth.

Before the Guests — Sauté cubes of sweetbread with mushrooms (sliced or whole) in the butter in blazer pan of chafing dish. Stir broth to assure mixing of cornstarch and add to contents of blazer pan. Stir gently and continue cooking until sauce is clear (and cornstarch well cooked). Serve with shredded coconut on the side. Serves 4.

Tray-Maid	*Menu*
1) butter	Watercress and Melon Ball Salad
2) sweetbreads, diced	(or canned Queen Anne
3) mushrooms	Cherry Salad
4) broth, mixed with herbs and	according to season)
cornstarch	Sweetbread and
5) coconut	Mushroom Ragout
	Sliced Tomatoes and
	Green Onions
	Toasted Rolls
	Cream Cheese Bar le Duc
	and Crackers
	Coffee

Veal Rolls Maison in Burgundy

1 pound veal	salt and pepper
½ cup Virginia ham spread (about)	¼ cup drippings or butter
½ cup coarsely broken crackers	1 cup dry red wine
1 onion, finely minced	½ clove garlic
⅛ teaspoon marjoram	½ cup walnut or pecans, sliced
Kitchen Bouquet	paprika

Behind the Scenes — Purchase veal in very thin slices (as for veal parmigiana). Veal cut from the shin is preferred for this, although veal steaks are sometimes used. Cut into pieces about 3 x 4 inches in size making about 8 pieces. Spread each generously with Virginia ham spread. Mix rather coarsely broken cracker crumbs with minced onion and marjoram. Spread this over the ham spread. Roll up meat carefully (as you would a jelly roll) and skewer or tie each into place. Brush outside of meat rolls with Kitchen Bouquet. Have walnuts sliced and ready.

Before the Guests — Melt drippings or butter in blazer pan of chafing dish. Sprinkle veal rolls with salt and pepper and then brown in hot drippings. Toast the sliced walnuts or pecans in these drippings and then set aside. Spear the garlic on a toothpick and drop into blazer pan. Add wine. Bring almost to bubbling and then return all the veal rolls to the pan. Cover and cook well for about 20 minutes. Then sprinkle whole surface generously with paprika. Toss toasted nuts over top. Remove garlic and serve with toast. Serves 2 to 4.

Tray-Maid	*Menu*
1) butter or drippings	Citrus Fruit Salad
2) veal rolls, ready to cook	(with lemon juice dressing
3) sliced nuts	and plenty of mint)
4) garlic on toothpick	Veal Rolls Maison in Burgundy
5) wine	with Toast Points
6) paprika	Stuffed Celery
7) toast	Molded Pineapple Rice Pudding
8) salt and pepper	Coffee

Frogs' Legs Provençal

3 pairs (small) frogs' legs
Kitchen Bouquet
salt and pepper
½ cup butter
½ clove garlic
dash of dried thyme
dash of orégano
1 tomato, skinned, cut fine
½ cup white wine

Behind the Scenes — Frogs' legs must be skinned (this is generally done at the shop). If you must do it, note that the skin turns back and pulls off like a kid glove. Brush with Kitchen Bouquet. Sprinkle with salt and pepper. Scald, skin and cut up tomato.

Before the Guests — Melt butter in blazer pan of chafing dish. Spear garlic (cut into halves) on toothpick and drop into butter. Sauté frogs' legs until beginning to brown (about 10 minutes), then add remaining ingredients. Cook uncovered, basting until frogs' legs are cooked through (25 to 30 minutes). Serves 3 to 4.

Tray-Maid	*Menu*
1) butter	Liver Pâté with Toast Points
2) frogs' legs, prepared for cooking	Frogs' Legs Provençal
	Green Noodles
3) garlic on toothpick	(spinach noodles)
4) thyme	Watercress
5) orégano	Raspberries in Port
6) tomato, skinned & cut	Macaroons
7) wine	Coffee

Lamb with the Syrian Touch

1 pound lamb, cubed
2 green peppers
1 onion
1 stalk celery
1 clove garlic, minced
½ teaspoon salt

2 tablespoons butter or drippings
½ teaspoon Kitchen Bouquet
½ cup water
¼ cup red wine
  cayenne or Tabasco
½ cup pine nuts

Behind the Scenes — Purchase a pound piece of lamb shoulder; have it boned and cut into cubes about an inch in size. Salt and pepper meat, brush with Kitchen Bouquet, and dust lightly with flour. Cut tops off green peppers and seed. Parboil in ½ cup water about 5 minutes (save water). Then cut peppers into inch squares. Cut celery into squares. Cut the onion lengthwise into small pieces. Mince garlic, add salt and with flat side of knife rub garlic to a paste.

Before the Guests — Melt drippings in blazer pan of chafing dish. Sauté the lamb cubes in this until lightly browned. Add remaining ingredients with pine nuts sprinkled over top near end of cooking. Cover. Simmer 10 minutes. Serve with boiled rice. Serves 2 to 4.

Tray-Maid

1) butter
2) lamb, cubed and floured
3) green peppers, parboiled and squared
4) celery, squared
5) onions, sliced
6) garlic, rubbed to a paste
7) wine
8) water from peppers
9) cayenne or Tabasco
10) pine nuts

Menu

Tossed Green Salad
Lamb with the Syrian Touch
Fluffy Rice
Crisp Crusted Rolls
Rum Cake   Coffee

Jiggs' Favorite

        1 can corned beef (12 ounces)
        1 onion, minced
        2 tablespoons American red
            wine
        1 bay leaf, crushed
        ½ teaspoon caraway seed
        2 cups very finely shredded cab-
            bage
        ½ cup water
            freshly ground pepper

Behind the Scenes — Just set out all the ingredients, opening can of corned beef, mincing onion, and shredding cabbage very, very finely.   Red and white cabbage make a handsome combination to serve.

Before the Guests — Heat together the corned beef and onion in blazer pan of chafing dish, directly over the flame.   When piping hot, add wine, crushed bay leaf and caraway seeds. Cover.   When bubbling and steaming, add cabbage.   Heat to piping hot.   Cook 3 minutes and serve at once.   Serves 4 to 6.

Tray-Maid	*Menu*
1) corned beef	Waldorf Salad
2) minced onion	Jiggs' Favorite with
3) wine	Mashed or Riced Potatoes or
4) crushed bay leaf	Potatoes Boiled in Jackets
5) caraway seeds	Green Onions
6) cabbage, shredded and pre- cooked	Cheese and Crackers
	Beer

Veal Kidneys in White Wine

2 veal kidneys
6 green onions, chopped finely
6 mushrooms, sliced
2 tablespoons parsley, minced
4 tablespoons butter
2 tablespoons brandy
salt and pepper
½ cup white wine
1 teaspoon heavy meat jelly

Behind the Scenes — Slice kidneys and remove the membrane and suet. Chop the onions (top included), wash and slice mushrooms. Mince parsley.

Before the Guests — Melt butter in blazer pan of chafing dish. When sizzling, add sliced kidneys. Cook over high flame, as kidneys must cook quickly. This should take about 5 minutes. Lower flame; pour brandy over kidneys; set aflame. When blaze goes out, add onions, mushrooms and parsley. Blend well, seasoning with salt and pepper. Add wine and cook 10 minutes. Add meat jelly and allow to melt and blend before serving. (Note—if you have Glace de Viande, which is a heavy meat jelly, you may add it to this dish, but it is entirely optional.) Serves 2.

Tray-Maid	*Menu*
1) butter	Hot Vegetable Bouillon
2) sliced kidneys	Veal Kidneys in White Wine
3) brandy	Riced Potatoes
4) onions, chopped	Spiced Peaches in Sauce
5) mushrooms, sliced	Coffee
6) parsley, minced	
7) salt and pepper	
8) wine	
9) meat jelly (optional)	

Squabs Delice

2 squabs (1 to 1½ pounds each)
  Kitchen Bouquet
  thyme
  onion salt
  fine crumbs
¼ cup butter
2 tablespoons shortening

8 green onions (with tops)
  minced
1 tomato, skinned and minced
½ cup California white wine
¼ cup grated cheese
½ cup sour cream

Behind the Scenes — When purchasing birds, have them split and the breast bone removed. Have them pounded flat. Brush with Kitchen Bouquet. Rub with powdered thyme and onion salt. Spread with butter, then dust lightly with crumbs. Mince onions; skin and mince the tomato. Measure wine, cheese and sour cream.

Before the Guests — Note that this dish takes time to prepare: therefore, be sure to serve hors d'oeuvres that will keep the guests occupied while your cooking goes on. Melt shortening in blazer pan of chafing dish. Brown birds in this, one at a time. Add onion and tomato to drippings. Add wine and cover. When sauce almost reaches the bubbling point, return birds to blazer pan. Cook until well done (this will take almost thirty minutes), basting from time to time with the sauce. Sprinkle cheese over top about 5 minutes before finishing. Transfer to serving plate. Add sour cream to sauce in pan; remove from heat. Stir to mix and serve at once around the birds. Serves 2 to 4.

Tray-Maid	*Menu*
1) shortening	Hot Hors d'Oeuvres
2) squabs, prepared for cooking	Squabs Delice with Wild Rice
3) minced onion	Asparagus Tips
4) minced tomato	Spumoni
5) wine	Coffee
6) cheese	
7) sour cream	

Kidney Beans Chili—Surprise

1 can red kidney beans
6 slices bacon, minced
1 teaspoon chili powder
2 green peppers
   3-ounce package cream cheese
1 onion, minced
   corn bread

Behind the Scenes — Bake a pan of corn bread (no sugar in the mixture) and make it a thin crusty bread. Cut into squares *while hot.* It can be *served cold* or toasted in electric toaster at serving time. Cut tops off green peppers. Remove seeds; parboil 5 minutes. Drain. Cool. Cut cream cheese into halves, lengthwise, and place half inside each pepper. Put top in place and fasten with toothpicks. Mince bacon, mince onion. Turn kidney beans into bowl.

Before the Guests — Sauté bacon bits with onion in blazer pan of chafing dish until crisp and beginning to brown. Place green peppers in the pan, turning them over on their sides. Cover and simmer about 10 minutes. Add chili powder to kidney beans (to taste). Pour beans over top of green peppers. Cover and cook 20 minutes at least, or until whole dish is piping hot. Serves 2.

Tray-Maid	*Menu*
1) bacon bits	Tossed Salad
2) minced onion	Kidney Beans Chili—Surprise
3) peppers, stuffed	Toasted Corn Bread Squares
4) kidney beans	Hot Apple Sauce
5) chili powder	Hot Apple Sauce with
6) corn bread for toasting	Whipped Cream
	Coffee

Beef Viennese with Stuffed Mushrooms

4 thin slices (3" x 4" size) of tender beef
½ pound medium-sized mushrooms
garlic
Kitchen Bouquet
liver pâté (or liver sausage)

hickory-smoked salt
freshly ground pepper
4 tablespoons butter
2 tablespoons Worcestershire sauce
lemon juice to taste

Behind the Scenes — Brush the serving-size pieces of beef with Kitchen Bouquet or Gravy Secret. Rub with cut side of clove of garlic. Then spread meat with a layer of liver pâté. Fold the meat over just once, pocketbook fashion; fasten with toothpick. Remove stems from mushrooms, chop these fine and mix with enough of the liver pâté to make a filling for the mushroom caps. Fill mushroom caps.

Before the Guests — Rub meat with smoked salt, sprinkle with freshly ground pepper. Melt butter in blazer pan of chafing dish. Sauté meat and then mushrooms until brown. Remove to serving platter. Add Worcestershire sauce to drippings in pan and then add lemon juice to taste. Pour over meat and mushrooms. Serves 2.

Tray-Maid

1) butter
2) meat, prepared and folded
3) hickory-smoked salt
4) mushrooms, stuffed
5) Worcestershire sauce
6) lemon

Menu

Hot Spiced Bouillon
with Cheese Crackers
Beef Viennese with
Stuffed Mushrooms
Thinly Sliced Salty Rye Bread
Baked Bananas and Coconut
Coffee

Spaghetti with Butter Sauce and Parmesan Cheese

1 pound spaghetti
½ cup butter
1 clove garlic
1 teaspoon salt
½ cup red wine
¼ teaspoon orégano
¼ teaspoon dry basil (or sprig of
    fresh)
½ cup grated Parmesan cheese
watercress

Behind the Scenes — Spaghetti may be boiled "el dente" beforehand. Place in a colander. Then just before serving time bring pot of water to boiling and quick as a wink dip the colander into the fast-boiling water, allow it to remain just long enough to reheat the spaghetti (not one minute longer), and drain; turn into a large, heated serving bowl. Rub the minced garlic with the salt until it forms a paste.

Before the Guests — Melt butter in blazer pan of chafing dish. Add the garlic, salt, red wine, and the herbs. Bring to bubbling. Simmer 3 minutes. Pour over hot spaghetti. Toss with large wooden fork and spoon, until well mixed. Add cheese; again toss until well mixed. Then just before serving toss in crisp sprigs of watercress (a generous bunch). Serve at once. Serves 4.

Tray-Maid	*Menu*
1) butter	Onion Soup
2) garlic	Spaghetti with Butter Sauce
3) salt	and Parmesan Cheese
4) red wine	Green Salad
5) herbs (check ingredients)	French Bread
6) cheese	Biscuit Tortoni
7) watercress	Coffee
8) spaghetti, kept warm	

White Monkey with Seedless Grapes

1 cup bread crumbs
1 cup milk
1 egg
2 tablespoons butter
1 cup sharp American cheese
  shredded
½ teaspoon salt
½ teaspoon dry mustard

cayenne pepper
2 bunches seedless Thompson
  grapes
4 squares shredded wheat
  "bites"
paprika or curry powder
garlic salt

Behind the Scenes — Soak bread crumbs in the milk. Add egg. Cut grapes in halves. Sprinkle shredded wheat squares with garlic salt (dot with butter, if desired). Toast, then sprinkle with paprika (or lightly with curry powder).

Before the Guests — Melt butter in blazer pan of chafing dish over direct flame. Remove and place over hot water and add cheese. When cheese is melted add milk with crumbs, salt, mustard, dash of cayenne. Stir vigorously for a minute. Arrange an attractive pile of the grape halves in center of each serving plate. Place one piece of the shredded toast beside it. Pour the monkey over the top, leaving tip of toast and tip of grapes to show on the side. Serves 2.

Tray-Maid

1) butter
2) cheese
3) bread crumbs, prepared
4) salt
5) mustard
6) cayenne
7) grapes, halved
8) shredded wheat squares, prepared

Menu

Antipasto
White Monkey with
White Grapes
Shredded Wheat Squares
Babas au Rhum
Coffee

Breast of Duck Flambée

breast of duck, raw or cooked
(from 1 or 2 ducks, depending upon size)
1 bottle hearts of artichokes
garlic
¼ cup butter or duck fat
¼ cup orange juice
¼ cup American red wine
½ teaspoon salt
1 bay leaf, crushed fine
⅛ teaspoon marjoram
1 small (hostess size) can black
cherries
1 tablespoon cornstarch
2 tablespoons brandy, cognac or
Kirsch

Behind the Scenes — Breast of duck may be taken from pre-roasted birds when other parts are to be used at another time. Breast meat may be sliced from frame, remainder of bird to be simmered or quickly roasted for some other serving. Slice into serving thickness, as necessary. Size of artichoke bottle or can ,depends upon number of people to be served. Open can; save liquid. Open can of cherries. Mix cornstarch with a little cold water to make a liquid paste.

Before the Guests — Rub inside of blazer pan well with a cut side of the garlic. Then add butter or duck fat and heat to bubbling. Add artichokes with just enough of their liquid to make heating easy. Remove them from pan, season with a little lemon juice and set aside to keep warm.

Again bring drippings in blazer pan to bubbling and sauté breast of duck until piping hot and cooked to preferred degree. Transfer to another pan to keep hot. Add remaining ingredients except cornstarch and simmer until reduced to savory sauce. Stir in the cornstarch. Continue stirring until sauce is clear and rich. Return breast of duck to pan; add cherries and arrange attractively. Border with the artichokes. Reheat if necessary. Pour brandy over top; set aflame. When flame dies down, serve at once with toast points, black olives, radish roses and potatoes julienne.

Tray-Maid

1) garlic
2) butter or duck fat
3) artichokes and liquid
4) salt and pepper
5) breast of duck
6) orange juice
7) wine
8) bay leaf
9) marjoram
10) cherries
11) cornstarch
12) brandy, cognac, Kirsch

Menu

Shrimp Cocktail
Breast of Duck Flambée
Black Olives   Radish Roses
Julienne Potatoes
Halves of Melon with Lime Ice
Coffee

Deviled Crab Cakes with Cucumber Sauce

1 can condensed cream of mushroom soup
1 teaspoon dry mustard
dash of cayenne
1 tablespoon parsley, minced
3 cups cooked or canned crabmeat

2 egg yolks
½ cup dry fine bread crumbs
1 egg beaten with 1 tablespoon
of water
4 tablespoons butter or margarine
cucumber sauce

Behind the Scenes — Combine the mushroom soup with mustard, cayenne, parsley, crabmeat and egg yolks. Chill thoroughly. While the crab mixture is chilling make the cucumber sauce. Peel, seed, and dice one cucumber. Mince one onion and mince 1 teaspoon of parsley. Combine these with 2 cups of tomato pulp, ½ teaspoon salt, ½ teaspoon paprika and dash of pepper in saucepan. Simmer about 20 minutes. Add 1 tablespoon tarragon vinegar and mix until blended. Keep warm until serving time.

When crab mixture is chilled form into cakes. Beat the egg with the water and dip crab cakes first in crumbs, then into egg, and again into crumbs.

Before the Guests — Melt butter in blazer pan of chafing dish. When sizzling hot sauté the crab cakes to a golden brown on both sides. Remove to a hot platter and keep warm until all cakes are cooked. Serve with cucumber sauce and garnish with watercress. Serves 6.

Tray-Maid

1) butter
2) crab cakes
3) watercress
4) cucumber sauce kept hot over
boiling water

Menu

Minted Fruit Cup
Crab Cakes with
Cucumber Sauce
Green Beans Julienne
with Almonds
Hot Parker House Rolls
Coffee Ice Cream
Coffee

Chicken Rex—Double Decker

2 cups cooked chicken (about 1 pound)
4-ounce can button mushrooms
1 stalk celery, cut julienne
10½-ounce can chicken broth
2 tablespoons cornstarch
⅛ teaspoon powdered sage
⅛ teaspoon powdered thyme
2 tablespoons butter
1 cup whipped cream
⅛ teaspoon nutmeg
12 pastry squares (or 6 patty shells)

Behind the Scenes — Drain liquid from mushrooms and add to chicken broth. Cut chicken into long strips. Cut the celery julienne and cook in small amount of salted water until just tender. Add celery water to chicken broth. Mix cornstarch and herbs with the broth.

To prepare pastry squares, use prepared pastry mix sufficient to make 2-crust pie. Mix as directed on box. Roll pastry ⅛ inch thick and cut into 3 inch squares (or use large cookie cutter and cut into rounds). Arrange on cookie sheet. Prick the pastry with a fork; then cover with a second cookie sheet. (This is to prevent the pastry from curling during baking.) Bake in hot oven (400° F.) about 8 minutes. Remove covering cooking sheet and let pastry brown. Remove to plate and set aside until serving time. Mix whipped cream with nutmeg.

Before the Guests — Stir broth in blazer pan over flame. Cook until rich, clear, and creamy. Add butter and adjust seasoning with salt or pepper, as needed. Add chicken, celery, mushrooms. Heat together until piping hot. Serve between and over the top of two layers of delicate pastry. Top with whipped cream. Garnish with parsley or watercress. (Or fill patty shells and top with whipped cream.) Serves 6.

Tray-Maid	*Menu*
1) chicken, mushroom, celery mixed	Fresh Fruit Cup with Grenadine
	Chicken Rex
2) broth mixed with cornstarch and herbs	Broccoli Vinaigrette
	Beaten Biscuits
3) butter	Custard Pie
4) whipped cream	Coffee
5) pastry or patty shells	

Beef and Oyster au Vin

        4 fillet of beef slices (rounds 1
            inch thick)
          Kitchen Bouquet
          garlic
       12 oysters
        3 tablespoons butter
        1 tablespoon cornstarch
        ½ cup oyster liquor
        ¼ teaspoon salt
        3 tablespoons port wine

Behind the Scenes — Pound the fillet steaks to make them slightly thinner; brush both sides with Kitchen Bouquet, then rub with cut side of garlic. Turn oysters into a sieve and drain, saving liquor. Run fingers through oysters to remove any bits of shell. Mix oyster liquor (add water to make ½ cup, if necessary) with cornstarch.

Before the Guests — Melt butter in blazer pan over flame. When piping hot, brown steaks quickly on both sides. Remove to serving platter to keep hot. Put oysters in pan and cook until edges curl. Transfer to the serving platter. Stir cornstarch in oyster liquor; pour into blazer pan. Stir until sauce is clear and rich and the cornstarch is completely cooked. Add salt and port wine. Heat quickly; pour over the oysters. Sprinkle steaks with salt and pepper, top with oysters, serve at once. Serves 4

Tray-Maid	*Menu*
1) butter	Pomegranate Halves with
2) fillets	Crisp Crackers
3) oysters	Beef and Oysters Au Vin
4) oyster liquor mixed with	Green Onions Baked Tomatoes
cornstarch	Apple Pie Cheese
5) salt and pepper	Coffee
6) port wine	

> 6 to 8 halves of cooked sweet
>   potatoes (yams)
> ½ cup butter
> ½ cup sugar
> ½ cup sherry
> ¼ teaspoon nutmeg
> ¼ teaspoon cinnamon
> ¼ cup shredded pineapple with
>   juice
> ¼ cup brown sugar
> 1 cup coarsely chopped pecans
> 2 to 3 tablespoons brandy

Behind the Scenes — Boil 3 to 4 large, sugary sweet (yam type) potatoes. Cool and skin and cut in halves. Mix the brown sugar with coarsely chopped pecans.

Before the Guests — Make a syrup in the blazer pan of the chafing dish, mixing butter, sugar, sherry, nutmeg, cinnamon and pineapple. Thin with hot water, if necessary, to obtain proper consistency. Cook sweet potatoes in this sauce, two or three halves at a time, until well heated through, setting each aside where it will keep warm until all are browned. Then return all to the blazer pan. Sprinkle mixture of brown sugar and pecans over top. Pour brandy over this and set aflame. When flame dies down, serve at once. Serves 4 to 6 (depending on size of sweet potatoes).

Tray-Maid	*Menu*
1) sweet potato halves	Melon Halves with Lime Juice
2) brown sugar and pecans	Sweet Potatoes—Delight
3) butter	with Delicate Cold Cuts
4) sugar	Celery Stuffed with Liver Pâté
5) sherry	Berry Tarts
6) nutmeg	Coffee
7) cinnamon	
8) pineapple with juice	
9) brandy	

Blazing Ham Steak

2 pounds sliced smoked ham	1 tablespoon water
½ pound mushrooms	2 tablespoons butter
2 tablespoons curry powder	¼ cup consommé
1 tablespoon flour	¼ cup spiced brandied peaches,
2 tablespoons fine crumbs	chopped fine
¼ teaspoon pepper	¼ cup juice from the peaches
¼ teaspoon salt	2 tablespoons brandy
1 egg	

Behind the Scenes — Have the ham cut into thin steaks at market. At home, trim off the fat. Cut this fat into bits and save for later use. Cut steaks into 8 serving-size pieces. Mix seasoning, flour and crumbs. Mix egg with water. Dip ham in crumb mixture, then egg, then crumbs. Stem mushrooms. Slice stems. Use mushrooms whole if small enough.

Before the Guests — Melt butter in blazer pan of chafing dish. Then sauté prepared ham in this until pieces are delicately browned. Add mushrooms and brown; then add consomme. Cover and cook gently for 10 minutes. Add the spiced peaches and juice. Reheat. Pour brandy over top, set aflame. Serve as soon as flame dies out. Serves 6 to 8.

Tray-Maid

1) ham, prepared for sauté
2) mushrooms
3) butter
4) consommé
5) minced peaches with sauce
6) brandy

Menu

*Chilled Minted Cream Soup
Blazing Ham Steak—Curry
with Zucchini
Ice Box Cake
Coffee

* Combine two 10½ ounce cans cream of chicken and cream of pea soup. Thin with cream. Add fresh mint. Chill.

Supreme of Chicken Marjolaine

breast of 3½-pound chicken
¼ teaspoon nutmeg
½ teaspoon salt
⅛ teaspoon pepper
½ teaspoon rosemary, bay leaf, thyme, marjoram combined

½ cup butter
1 tablespoon lemon (or lime) juice
½ cup sherry
1½ cups cooked wild rice
minced parsley

Behind the Scenes — Trim the breast from chicken; cut into four slices. Mix together about ⅛ teaspoon of each of the herbs, crushing the bay leaf to fine bits. Roll all together to a well-blended fine seasoning. Add the salt, pepper, and nutmeg. Prepare wild rice and keep hot over hot water. Mince parsley.

Before the Guests — Rub the meat well with blended seasoning. Melt half the butter in the blazer pan of chafing dish. Sauté the pieces of chicken breast until cooked through and delicately browned. Remove from pan. Add remaining butter, lemon juice and sherry. Simmer gently to make a rich sauce. Return chicken to the sauce. Reheat gently. Serve with wild rice. Sprinkle with minced parsley. Serves two.

Tray-Maid	*Menu*
1) chicken breast on waxed paper	Vichyssoise
2) mixed seasonings	Supreme of Chicken Marjolaine
3) butter	with Wild Rice
4) ½ lemon, to be squeezed when needed	French Endive Toasted Rolls
5) sherry	Pears with Cheese
6) cooked rice, kept warm over hot water	Coffee

Poached Eggs Ranch Style

1 clove garlic
1 teaspoon orégano
1 chili pepper
1 cup tomato purée
3 tablespoons oil
1 cup tomato sauce
  salt and pepper
2 eggs per person

Behind the Scenes — Mash the garlic, orégano and chili pepper very finely.   Mix with the tomato purée and strain.

Before the Guests — Heat oil in blazer pan over flame.   Add the tomato purée, tomato sauce and salt and pepper.   Heat thoroughly.   Break eggs into sauce and poach to desired degree, basting with sauce as eggs cook.

Tray-Maid	*Menu*
1) oil	Poached Eggs Ranch Style
2) tomato purée, strained	Potato Salad Stuffed Celery
3) tomato sauce	Seeded Rolls
4) salt and pepper	Ice Box Cake
5) eggs	Coffee

Eggs Lyonnaise Amandine

    1 cup white wine
    2 tablespoons green onions,
        minced
    ½ cup almonds, blanched and
        slivered
    2 teaspoons cornstarch
    4 eggs
        toast
        paprika

Behind the Scenes — Mince onions, blanch and sliver almonds. Mix cornstarch with cold water to make a liquid paste.

Before the Guests — Heat wine in blazer pan over flame. Add onion and heat.   Break eggs into wine and poach to the degree of doneness desired.   Remove eggs from wine and transfer to hot buttered toast; keep warm.   Add almonds to sauce (reserving a few for garnish), then stir in cornstarch. Stir and cook until sauce is clear and rich (and cornstarch is cooked).   Pour sauce over eggs.   Top with a few slivered almonds and dust with paprika.   Serves 2 to 4.

Tray-Maid	*Menu*
1) onion, minced	Ham Spread Canapés
2) eggs	Eggs Lyonnaise Amandine
3) toast	Broccoli
4) almonds, blanched and slivered	Carrot Sticks
5) cornstarch	Pot de Crème Cookies
6) paprika	Coffee

B.Y.O.A.

CHAPTER NINE

LET'S NOT GO OUT

Perhaps it's pouring rain. Perhaps the Boss has tossed you a nasty look. Perhaps you're just plain pooped by the time you're home. Ah, *these* are moments when you wouldn't trade your chafing dish for all the uranium in the Congo! Pick up easy-to-prepare foods on your way home, or dig into cabinet and refrigerator supplies. Life will acquire a new cheerfulness!

Mushrooms Flambée

½ pound mushrooms (or an 8-
ounce can)
3 tablespoons butter
½ cup dry sherry or white wine
1 tablespoon lemon juice
⅛ teaspoon salt
dash pepper (or cayenne)
2 tablespoons brandy
¼ cup heavy cream
triangles of toast
minced parsley or chives

Behind the Scenes — Wash mushrooms, remove and slice stems. Use caps, sliced or whole.

At the Chafing Dish — Heat the shoestring potatoes in lower pan of chafing dish and cover to keep warm. Sauté mushrooms (stems and caps) in butter to light brown. Add wine and lemon juice, salt, pepper. Simmer until liquid is almost absorbed. Pour brandy over top and set aflame. When flame goes out, add cream. Reheat to bubbling. Serve on triangles of toast; add minced parsley for garnish. Serves 2.

Tray-Maid	*Menu*
1) mushrooms, sliced	Mushroom Flambée
2) butter	Shoestring Potatoes
3) seasonings	Cold Cuts
4) wine	French Endive
5) brandy	Tangerines Cookies
6) half lemon (squeeze juice into	Coffee
chafing dish when needed	
7) cream	
8) minced parsley	

Salisbury Steak

1 pound ground round steak
2 tablespoons lemon juice
2 tablespoons minced parsley
½ teaspoon celery seeds
½ teaspoon salt
pepper

meat coloring agent
1 package Minute Rice .
½ lemon
2 onions, thinly sliced
2 tablespoons butter
2 tablespoons catsup

Behind the Scenes — Mix round steak with 1 tablespoon of the lemon juice. Add parsley, celery seeds, salt, pepper. Shape into a large round patty that will just fit into blazer pan of chafing dish. Then brush both sides of the meat with meat coloring.

At the Chafing Dish — First cook the minute rice in the lower pan of your chafing dish. Cover tightly (as directed on package) and allow to finish cooking while meat is prepared.

Melt butter in blazer pan; when piping hot, slip meat patty into butter and brown meat first on one side, then the other side. Cook to degree preferred. Transfer to hot serving platter. Put onions into blazer pan in the drippings and sauté to brownness. Add remaining tablespoon of lemon juice and catsup. Heat. Serve over top or at side of steak patty. Serve with minute rice, which should now be ready.

Tray-Maid

1) butter
2) meat patty
3) half lemon, squeeze as needed
4) catsup
5) onions, sliced
6) rice

Menu

Sliced Oranges with Mint
Salisbury Steak with Onion Sauce
Minute Rice
Cheese with Crackers and
Fruit Wedges
Coffee

Pan Broiled Oysters

1 dozen oysters
4 tablespoons butter
paprika
lemon juice
salt
lima beans
sour cream
minced parsley
pepper
watercress
toast points

Behind the Scenes — Turn oysters into a strainer, saving the liquor. Run fingers through oysters to remove any bits of shell. Mince the parsley. Wash watercress and chill. Prepare bread for toast. Defrost limas or prepare as necessary.

At the Chafing Dish — First heat limas (see menu) in lower pan of chafing dish, seasoning with salt, pepper, and 2 to 3 tablespoons heavy or sour cream. Keep hot while oysters cook.

For oysters: Melt butter in blazer pan. When hot, add oysters and sauté gently until edges curl. Add generous sprinkling of paprika, juice of 1 lemon, oyster liquor, salt, pepper. Cover, cook for 2 to 3 minutes. Serve on toast points, sprinkle with minced parsley and garnish with watercress. Serves 2.

Tray-Maid	*Menu*
1) lima beans	Grapefruit and Fresh Grapes
2) seasonings	in a Fruit Cup
3) sour cream	Pan Broiled Oysters
4) oysters	with Lemon Sauce
5) oyster liquor	Tender Green Limas
6) butter	Celery
7) lemon, cut in halves	Spice Cake
8) parsley, minced	Coffee
9) watercress, crisped	
10) bread for toast points	

Frizzled Beef with Crumb Sauce and Grilled Tomatoes

½ pound dried beef
6 tablespoons butter or margarine
2 tablespoons fresh (but fine) bread crumbs

piece of cucumber
1 cup top milk (or thin cream)
¼ teaspoon Gravy Secret
2-3 hard-crusted rolls
6 thick slices tomatoes

Behind the Scenes — Rinse the dried beef; it may not be too salty, although, on the other hand, it is usually salty enough to spoil a fine dish. Drain well.

Cut off piece of cucumber about 1 inch long. Pare and cut into cubes.

Cut tops off hard-crusted rolls and scoop out the centers. Make soft crumbs of the centers for use in making the sauce later. Brush or spread inside of rolls with butter (rub surface of rolls with garlic, if desired). Toast rolls and keep warm. Slice tomatoes, season with garlic or onion salt. Dip in crumbs.

At the Chafing Dish — Melt 4 tablespoons of the butter in chafing dish and when piping hot add the dried beef. Sauté until delicately browned and well crisped. Push all the beef to one side of the pan. Tilt the pan slightly to collect the fat. Add the fine bread crumbs and toss until brown. Add the cucumber and the top milk. Stir until rich sauce is formed. Stir in the Gravy Secret. Fill the toasted cases made from the hard rolls.

Melt remaining 2 tablespoons butter in lower pan of chafing dish (or in blazer pan, just emptied). Brown tomato slices and serve with the beef.

Tray-Maid	*Menu*

Tray-Maid	*Menu*
1) dried beef (rinsed)	Pickled Artichokes
2) butter	Frizzled Beef with Crumb Sauce
3) bread crumbs	Grilled Tomatoes
4) hollowed-out rolls	Fig Pudding and Rum Sauce
5) cucumber, cubed	Coffee
6) top milk	
7) Gravy Secret	
8) sliced tomatoes, crumbed	

Salmon à la Reine

2 tablespoons butter
1 tablespoon flour
½ cup water
juice of lemon
dash of pepper
¼ teaspoon salt
small onion, finely minced
2 hard-cooked eggs
1-pound can salmon (or 1
pound fresh-boiled salmon)

Behind the Scenes — Salmon must be ready—boil it or open a tin of canned salmon. Mince the onion. Cook eggs (must be hard cooked). Separate yolks from white. Slice white into rings (ready for garnish). Rub egg yolks through a sieve.

At the Chafing Dish — Melt butter in blazer pan. Add flour; mix smooth. Add water, lemon juice, salt, onion and the egg yolk (reserving about 1 teaspoon for garnish later). Stir and cook to a sauce. Add salmon (keeping it in one piece, as far as possible) and heat through, basting with the sauce during the cooking. Garnish with rings of egg white. Serves 2 to 4.

Tray-Maid	*Menu*
1) salmon	Tossed Salad with
2) butter	Cream Dressing
3) flour	Salmon à la Reine
4) water	with Potato Soufflé
5) lemon juice	Broiled Grapefruit
6) onion, minced	Coffee
7) salt, pepper	
8) eggs, yolks sieved and whites sliced	

Lamb Kidney Sauté with Wine Sauce

6 lamb kidneys
salt and pepper
flour or crumbs
1 dozen blanched almonds
½ dozen stuffed olives
2 strips bacon
½ clove garlic
1 tomato (or 1 teaspoon tomato
     paste)
¼ to ½ cup white wine

Behind the Scenes — Cut lamb kidneys into halves. Rinse in boiling water; drain. Carefully trim out bits of fat and membrane. Salt, pepper and flour (or crumb) the halves. Blanch and skin almonds. Cut bacon strips into bits. Mash garlic to fine paste. Skin and cut tomato quite small.

At the Chafing Dish — Try out the bacon bits in blazer pan of chafing dish until crisp and brown. Add prepared kidneys and turn until delicately browned all over. Add almonds and brown. Add olives (whole or cut in pieces). Add garlic paste and tomato. Add wine. Simmer gently until blended. Then continue until sauce is of desired consistency. Adjust seasoning with additional salt and pepper, if necessary. Occasionally a dash of sugar is necessary.

Tray-Maid	*Menu*
1) kidneys, prepared	Lamb Kidney Sauté
2) almonds, blanched and	with Wine Sauce
skinned	Baked Potatoes
3) olives, whole or cut in pieces	Banana Flambée
4) bacon, cut fine	(To be prepared later in same
5) garlic, mashed to paste	chafing dish—see recipe, page 231)
6) tomato, cut small	
7) white wine	

Curried Shad Roe

   1 tablespoon olive oil
   1 small onion, minced
   1 teaspoon curry
  ⅛ teaspoon cayenne
   2 tablespoons heavy cream
   1 tablespoon vinegar
   1 shad roe (or 1 can of shad roe)

Behind the Scenes — Parboil roe gently in salted water with 1 tablespoon of vinegar for 5 minutes. Plunge into cold water; drain and cool. Slice. (Or open tin of shad roe.) Mince onion.

At the Chafing Dish — Heat oil in blazer pan. Sauté onion until tender. Add curry, cayenne and cream. Arrange slices of roe in sauce and heat thoroughly, basting from time to time with the sauce. Serve piping hot. Serves 2.

Tray-Maid	*Menu*
1) olive oil	Avocado Canapés
2) roe slices	Curried Shad Roe
3) onion, minced	Green Peas
4) curry	Mixed Green Salad
5) cayenne	Poppy Seed Bread
6) cream	Fresh Pears with Cheese
	Coffee

Crabmeat with Sherry

3 tablespoons butter
3 tablespoons flour
1 cup milk
½ cup cream
1 tablespoon Worcestershire
   sauce
¼ teaspoon dry mustard
½ teaspoon salt

⅛ teaspoon freshly ground pepper
1 tablespoon paprika
1 cup fresh crabmeat (or 8-
   ounce can)
3 tablespoons sherry
toast rounds
parsley

Behind the Scenes — Run fingers carefully through crabmeat to remove any cartilage or shell. Flake coarsely. Measure flour onto waxed paper. Measure butter into blazer pan. Measure milk and cream.

At the Chafing Dish — Melt butter in blazer pan of chafing dish. Blend in flour. Add milk and cream; cook, stirring constantly until mixture thickens. Add Worcestershire sauce, dry mustard and salt and pepper. Fold in crabmeat. Heat thoroughly. Just before removing from flame add sherry. Serve on toast rounds; sprinkle with paprika and garnish with parsley clusters. Serves 4.

Tray-Maid	*Menu*
1) butter	Consommé Julienne
2) flour	Crabmeat with Sherry
3) milk	Spinach Salad with
4) cream	Tart Dressing
5) Worcestershire	Cherries Flambée
6) mustard	Coffee
7) seasonings	
8) crabmeat	
9) sherry	
10) toast rounds	
11) parsley	

Scotch Woodcock

2 tablespoons butter
4 eggs
1 tablespoon water
1 tablespoon capers
½ teaspoon salt
⅛ teaspoon pepper
2 slices buttered toast
anchovy paste

Behind the Scenes — No preparation for this *chafing dish special*. Have your toaster at hand for freshly made toast.

At the Chafing Dish — Melt butter in blazer pan, then place over hot water. Break eggs into the pan, stirring immediately to mix them well. Add water, capers, salt and pepper to taste. Stir over the hot water until eggs are fluffy and scrambled to your preferred degree of moistness. Have freshly made toast ready; butter and spread with anchovy paste. Serve the scrambled eggs on this toast. Add 1 or 2 strips of anchovies to top of each, if desired. Serves 2.

Note: Pan-broil several slices of drained canned pineapple in saucepan immediately after woodcock is served.

Tray-Maid	*Menu*
1) eggs	Scotch Woodcock
2) water	Broiled Pineapple
3) butter	Toast Coffee
4) capers	
5) salt and pepper	
6) toast	
7) anchovy paste	
8) pineapple slices, if desired	

Deviled Roe

1 small can (4 to 5 ounces) fish
  roe
2 tablespoons butter or margarine
½ teaspoon prepared mustard
  dash dried basil or orégano
  toast
  sliced lemon

Behind the Scenes — Nothing! Except to open a small tin of fish roe. These tins vary in size and contain roe from herring or from some other less important fish. These are very good and inexpensive (shad roe may be purchased in cans but are fairly expensive).

At the Chafing Dish — Heat bouillon (see menu) in blazer pan before preparation of roe, or heat in lower pan of chafing dish and keep hot until serving time. Melt butter or margarine in blazer pan of chafing dish. Add herb and prepared mustard. Add roe and sauté gently until heated through, turning in the sauce from time to time, or basting roe with sauce. Serve on hot buttered toast with slice of lemon. Serves 1 to 2.

Tray-Maid	*Menu*
1) fish roe	Hot Tomato Bouillon
2) butter	Deviled Roe
3) prepared mustard	Cabbage and Green Pepper Slaw
4) herbs	Quartered Tomatoes
5) bread to toast	Rolls—Jam
6) lemon	Fresh Fruit in Season
	Coffee

Oysters à la Crème

        1 dozen oysters
        2 tablespoons butter
        ⅛ teaspoon salt
          dash pepper
          dash nutmeg
        ½ bay leaf
        1 cup cream
          toast

Behind the Scenes — Drain oysters and save liquor. Run fingers through the oysters to remove all bits of shell.

At the Chafing Dish — Melt butter in blazer pan of chafing dish. Add oysters and liquor and seasonings. Simmer gently until edges of oysters curl. Add cream. Heat gently to bubbling. Serve at once on toast. Serves 2.

Tray-Maid	*Menu*
1) butter	Waldorf Salad
2) oysters	Oysters a la Crème
3) liquor	with Toast
4) salt, pepper and nutmeg	Hearts of Celery
5) bay leaf	Ice Cream
6) cream	Coffee
7) toast	

Chicken Livers Rosemary

1 pound chicken livers
2 tablespoons butter
½ cup white wine (sauterne, Rhine wine, etc.)
⅛ teaspoon rosemary
½ teaspoon salt
⅛ teaspoon freshly ground pepper

Behind the Scenes — Wash and dry chicken livers. Prepare rice in lower pan of chafing dish. Prepare cheese puffs; have ready to pop into oven while chicken livers are cooking.

At the Chafing Dish — Melt butter in blazer pan of chafing dish. When sizzling drop chicken livers in. Season with salt and pepper and sprinkle with rosemary. Cook quickly until well browned (about 10 minutes). Add wine and simmer another 10 minutes. Serve over rice or on the side. Serves 4.

Tray-Maid	*Menu*
	Cheese Puffs
1) chicken livers	Chicken Livers Rosemary
2) butter	Turkish Rice
3) seasonings	Raw Vegetable Salad
4) rosemary	Marrons Glacés
5) wine	Coffee

Broiled Liver with Creamed Corn

> 4 small pieces calf or lamb liver
> Kitchen Bouquet
> onion salt
> fine dry crumbs
> 8-ounce can cream-style corn
>   or 1 cup fresh corn
> 2 stuffed olives
> 2 tablespoons heavy cream
> salt and pepper
> dash of sugar

Behind the Scenes — Brush liver with Kitchen Bouquet; sprinkle with salt and pepper, and dip in crumbs. Open tin of corn or cut fresh corn from cob, to make 1 cup pulp.

At the Chafing Dish — If you have a one-pan chafing dish, the corn can be cooked quickly after liver is completed, since it requires little time. If you have a two-pan dish, then place corn, cream, olives, sugar, and seasonings in lower pan of chafing dish and heat to bubbling, or until fresh corn is cooked. Cover and keep warm.

Melt butter or bacon drippings in blazer pan. Sauté liver in this to desired degree of doneness. Serves 2.

Tray-Maid	*Menu*
1) liver, prepared	Consommé Madrilene
2) corn, already mixed with seasonings & cream	Broiled Liver with Creamed Corn
	Cole Slaw
	Fruit and Coffee

Potatoes Lyonnaise with Corned Beef

6 medium-sized cold boiled po-
    tatoes
3 onions, finely chopped
2 tablespoons butter
salt and pepper
12-ounce tin corned beef

Behind the Scenes — The potatoes are best when they are cooked in their jackets. Cool; skin and slice quite thin. (Or slice leftover boiled potatoes.) Mince onion. Remove corned beef from tin.

At the Chafing Dish — Melt butter in blazer pan. Add onion and sauté to light brownness. Add potatoes, sprinkle with salt and pepper. Press down with fork or spatula into hot onions and butter. Do not disturb until brown on bottom; then turn with spatula, again pressing down firmly on bottom of blazer. Continue until potatoes are well browned and piping hot. Remove to serving platter. Turn corned beef into blazer pan at once. Heat through quickly. Serve with the potatoes. Add a snappy relish or chili sauce in the serving.

Tray-Maid	*Menu*
1) sliced potatoes	Relish
2) minced onion	Potatoes Lyonnaise
3) butter	with Corned Beef
4) salt and pepper	Tossed Salad
5) corned beef	Sliced Tomatoes with
6) relish	Chopped Fresh Basil
	Rum Crème
	Coffee

Steak in a Chafing Dish

    3-minute steaks
    Kitchen Bouquet
  2 tablespoons butter
  2 onions, minced
  3 or 4 walnuts
  2 teaspoons mustard
  1 teaspoon Worcestershire sauce
  2 tablespoons chili sauce
  2 tablespoons sherry

Behind the Scenes — Mince onion and slice the nuts. If frozen steaks are used they may be set out of refrigerator to begin to thaw, but thawing is not necessary. Brush both sides of steaks with Kitchen Bouquet.

At the Chafing Dish — Heat butter in blazer pan, over flame. When piping hot, add steaks and brown quickly on both sides. Remove to serving platter. Add onion and nuts and sauté quickly. Add remaining ingredients and bring to boil quickly. Serve with steak. Serves 2.

Tray-Maid	*Menu*
1) steaks brushed with Kitchen Bouquet	Liver Pâté
	Steak in a Chafing Dish
2) onion, minced	Corn Pudding
3) walnuts, sliced	French Rolls Preserves
4) butter	Fruit Cheese
5) mustard	Coffee
6) Worcestershire	
7) chili sauce	
8) sherry	

B.Y.O.A.

B.Y.O.A.

CHAPTER TEN

DESSERTS

We know one gourmet who solemnly states that the boundaries of civilization are marked with the flames of *crêpes suzette*. Be that as it may, the desserts made possible by the chafing dish are certainly the most civilized morsels available to sinful man. Zabaglione . . . Flaming Cherries Jubilee . . . Royale Peaches Aflame—these are names to stir the blood. Make them! Strangers will whisper your name with awe, and monarchs vie for your attention.

Zabaglione

6 egg yolks
2 tablespoons sugar
½ cup wine (your choice of any
    white wine, Madeira or Mar-
    sala)

Behind the Scenes — Try out this show for the family before you begin to produce it on Broadway. It's an art to make a perfect zabaglione. Check the ingredients and you'll see this is really a custard made with wine instead of milk or cream. Like all custards it must never be overheated or the eggs will lump and separate. Your smooth custard will be gone with the wind (or heat). This wine custard must also be puffy as a cloud; consequently, it must be beaten constantly all through the cooking. Therefore get the correct tools for making zabaglione in a chafing dish. For beating, have a medium-sized wooden spoon at hand. Also secure one of those small wire whisks (the kind the French use). You will use the hot water pan of your chafing dish from start to finish but be sure to keep that water only medium hot. Keep a cup of cold water handy to tone down the temperature, if necessary. Don't let all these instructions confound you; follow directions and you'll wonder why anyone should say it is hard to make a good zabaglione. It's all in knowing how.

Zabaglione (Cont'd)

Before the Guests — Put the egg yolks, sugar and wine into blazer pan of chafing dish. With your wooden spoon mix them well together; even beat them together well. Then place the blazer pan over the hot water pan and begin to beat, using either the wooden spoon or the wire whisk. If the egg shows signs of forming little kernels, remove from over the hot water pan *at once* and beat until lumps disappear. Replace over hot water and continue beating steadily, steadily, steadily, until the custard puffs high and light and at the same time seems to be getting thicker. When it coats the spoon and begins to hold its shape as the spoon moves, then serve at once. This will serve from 4 to 6.

Tray-Maid

1) egg yolks
2) sugar
3) wine
4) check utensils

Dinner Service

Clear Soup
Lamb Kidneys Brochette
Shoestring Potatoes
Broccoli Vinaigrette
Zabaglione
Coffee

Rum Sabayon

½ cup sugar
6 egg yolks
3 cups American white wine
2 ounces rum (¼ cup)

Behind the Scenes — Note explanation of preparation under *Zabaglione*.

Before the Guests — Let water be heating in lower pan of chafing dish. Combine egg yolks and sugar in blazer pan away from hot water. Beat with wooden spoon until creamy. Add wine, then place blazer over hot water. Cook, beating constantly until thick. It should look like a fluffy sponge-cake mix. Add rum. Serve as a sauce or as a hot toddy.

Tray-Maid	*Dual Service*
1) egg yolks	*A Cake Eater's Delight:* Squares of
2) sugar	
3) wine	Angel Cake
4) rum	Sponge Cake
5) wooden spoon for stirring	Fruit Cake
6) wire whisk for beating	with Rum Sabayon Sauce. Garnish with nut halves or cherries glacé.
	Hot Toddy Service: Serve in punch cups with finger strips of fruit cake.

Beignets de Pommes (Apple Fritters)

2 tart apples
1 lemon
½ cup powdered sugar
½ cup brandy
flour
3 tablespoons butter
½ teaspoon powdered cinnamon

Behind the Scenes — Core, pare and slice the apples in thin round slices. Squeeze lemon. Combine the lemon juice, powdered sugar and brandy. When blended and sugar is dissolved place apple slices in this mixture. Allow to stand until they have acquired the desired taste. Drain and dust lightly with flour.

Before the Guests — Melt butter in blazer pan of chafing dish. When sizzling hot, sauté the apple slices on both sides to a delicate brown. Sprinkle with extra powdered sugar and cinnamon. Serve very hot. Serves 4.

Tray-Maid	*Informal Dinner*
1) apple slices	Wine with Crackers
2) butter	Shrimp Creole with
3) powdered sugar	Saffron Rice
4) cinnamon	Watercress Cucumber Salad
	Beignets de Pommes

Chocolate Puff Soufflé

½ package of semi-sweet choco-
    late morsels
1 cup milk
3 tablespoons sugar
⅛ teaspoon salt
1 teaspoon vanilla
3 eggs
    cream

Behind the Scenes — This simple but delicious dessert needs no beforehand preparation.

Before the Guests — Place the chocolate morsels and milk in blazer pan of chafing dish. Place blazer over hot water. Beat with a small wire beater or a silver fork until smooth. Add sugar, salt, vanilla. Beat the eggs in a separate bowl with rotary beater until very light and fluffy. Add to ingredients in blazer pan. Mix lightly. Cover and cook over hot water for 20 minutes without lifting cover. Remove from heat and serve immediately with cream. Serves 4.

Tray-Maid

1) chocolate morsels
2) milk
3) sugar
4) salt
5) vanilla
6) eggs
7) cream
8) rotary beater

Super-Service

Have some little tartlet pie shells ready to receive this rich and delicious dessert . . . or hollow out center of cupcakes, saving the cut-out piece as a top hat for the dessert. This amount would then serve 6 to 8 and even 10.

Macedoine of Fruits Flambée

   2 ripe pears
½ cup fresh pineapple diced
   1 peach quartered
½ cup fresh strawberries, whole
   1 banana, sliced
     lemon juice
     apricot sauce
     brioche
     rum

Behind the Scenes — Prepare apricot sauce by boiling together 2 cups dried apricots (soaked and softened in water) with 1½ cups of sugar for about 15 minutes (to a pulp). Then rub through a fine strainer. Prepare the fresh fruit. Sprinkle with lemon juice to prevent discoloring while standing. Cut brioche into small pieces.

Before the Guests — Place fruits and brioche pieces in blazer pan of chafing dish. Cover with apricot sauce. Heat through gently. When hot, pour rum over all and set ablaze. Serves 6 to 8.

Tray-Maid	*Supper Service*
1) prepared fruit	Black Bean Soup
2) brioche pieces	Avocado-Chicken Salad
3) apricot sauce	Macedoine of Fruits Flambée
4) rum	

Flaming Maple Sauce

½ cup maple sugar
¼ cup butter
½ cup rum

Behind the Scenes — Grate the sugar or soften (in a very "low heat" oven) and crumble.

Before the Guests — Melt maple sugar and butter in blazer pan of chafing dish. Add ¼ cup of rum and heat 5 minutes. Pour remaining rum over top and set ablaze. When flame dies out serve at once over ice cream or a pudding.

Tray-Maid	*Birthday Refreshments*
1) maple sugar	Birthday Cake
2) butter	Ice Cream Neapolitan with
3) rum	Flaming Maple Sauce
	Coffee Wine
	Liqueurs

Flaming Fresh Apricots

¼ cup light brown sugar
¼ cup light corn syrup
2 tablespoons butter
dash of mace
4 to 6 fresh apricots
¼ cup water
2 tablespoons apricot liqueur
¾ cup rum or Kirschwasser

Behind the Scenes — Blanch apricots in boiling water to loosen skins. Drain and peel.

Before the Guests — Combine sugar, mace, corn syrup, butter, water, in blazer pan of chafing dish. Stir gently over moderate flame until blended. Add apricot liqueur and ¼ cup of the rum. When heated through, add apricots (whole). Cook over moderate flame until apricots are glazed and the syrup is quite thick. Pour remaining rum over them and set ablaze. Serves 2 to 4.

Tray-Maid	*Dinner for Two*
1) butter	Sherry and Biscuits
2) brown sugar and mace	Broiled Salmon Steaks
3) corn syrup	New Potatoes and Peas Minted
4) rum	Tossed Green Salad
5) apricots	Flaming Fresh Apricots
6) apricot liqueur	Demi-tasse
7) water	

Pear Flambée au Port

8 pear halves (canned)
1 cup juice
½ cup granulated sugar
1 cup port wine
3 tablespoons cornstarch
  lemon juice to taste
  brandy

Behind the Scenes — Measure juice from pears; add water if necessary to make a cup. Mix sugar with cornstarch.

Before the Guests — Place pear juice, sugar, and cornstarch in blazer pan of chafing dish. Stir over flame until sauce is crystal clear and thickened. Add wine (and lemon juice, if desired). Reheat over hot water; add pears and cook for 10 minutes, until heated through. Pour brandy over top and set ablaze.

Tray-Maid	*Dessert Service*
1) pears and their liquor	Pear Flambée au Port with
2) sugar and cornstarch mixed	Snappy Cheddar on Finger-
3) port wine	length Pieces of Toast
4) lemon juice	Wine or Coffee
5) brandy	Brandy

Raspberry Madeira

1 pint thin cream
5 egg yolks
5 tablespoons granulated sugar
1 pint fresh raspberries (or 1
    package quick-frozen)
⅛ teaspoon salt
    sponge cake
    Madeira

Behind the Scenes — Mix cream with egg yolks. If quick-frozen raspberries are used, defrost and omit sugar from recipe. If fresh berries are used, wash, drain and pick over berries, discarding any bruised or crushed ones. Cut sponge cake (home made or purchased from store) into small serving size squares. Place in shallow dish and pour enough Madeira over to soak through the cake.

Before the Guests — Place cream and egg yolks in blazer pan of chafing dish over hot water. Stir continuously until custard coats the spoon. Add raspberries, sugar, and salt. Mix together gently. Reheat (take care not to overcook this dessert or it will separate). Pour over the Madeira soaked cake. Serves 6 to 8.

Tray-Maid

1) cream and egg yolks, mixed
2) sugar
3) raspberries
4) Madeira soaked sponge cake

Sunday Supper
(ready for any number of guests)

Sliced Cold Roast or Ham
with Snappy Sauce
Potato Salad
Rolls with Butter and
Homemade Preserves
Raspberry Madeira
Demi-tasse

Royale Peaches Aflame

½ cup port wine
½ cup currant jelly
½ cup sugar
2 teaspoons lemon juice
¼ teaspoon cinnamon
8 well-drained peach halves
   (canned)
brandy

Behind the Scenes — Just set up tray. Open can of peaches and drain.

Before the Guests — Combine the wine, jelly, sugar, lemon juice and cinnamon in the blazer pan of chafing dish. Heat, stirring frequently until the jelly melts and all ingredients are well blended. Place peaches in sauce, cut side down; prick with a fork. Simmer for 5 minutes, basting the peaches with the sauce. Just before serving pour brandy over top and set ablaze. Serve alone or as suggested below.

Tray-Maid

1) port wine
2) jelly
3) sugar
4) lemon juice
5) cinnamon
6) peaches
7) brandy

Party Service

This is a particularly dramatic way to serve economical refreshments to a group of 8 or more guests. Serve the flaming halves on squares of angel food cake as the flame begins to die down. Or serve over ice cream with cake on the side. Serve with tall tinkling glasses of wine and soda in the summertime and with demitasse in the wintertime.

Brandied Bananas with Green Grapes

                4 fully ripe firm bananas
                ½ pound seedless (Thompson)
                    grapes
                ½ cup butter
                    juice of 2 lemons
                1 cup sugar
                ¼ to ½ cup brandy
                    ladyfingers, toasted

Behind the Scenes — Select bananas that are short and "chunky" in size. Remove skins. Cut into halves lengthwise. Cut grapes into halves.

Before the Guests — Melt butter in blazer pan of chafing dish. Arrange banana halves in this; sprinkle part of the sugar over top; add lemon juice. Turn the bananas as they cook, adding sugar gradually until all is used. When bananas are cooked and beginning to brown, add grapes. Toss these in the sauce gently. Pour brandy over top. Set ablaze. When flame dies down, blow it out (the sugar can keep it smoldering for some time). Serve on individual dessert plates with toasted ladyfingers. Serves 4.

Tray-Maid

1) bananas, prepared (with sprinkling of extra lemon juice to prevent their turning brown)
2) grapes, split
3) butter
4) lemon juice, squeezed and in a covered container (to protect vitamin C)
5) sugar
6) brandy
7) ladyfingers

Supper Service

Since the dessert is a stout one:

Jellied Madrilene with
Sprigs of Watercress
Cold Cuts
Artichokes with
Wine Butter Sauce
Brandied Bananas with
Green Grapes
Coffee

Flaming Brandy Sauce for Steamed Pudding

1 cup seedless raisins
1 cup brandy
1 cup water
1 cup sugar
¼ teaspoon salt
1½ tablespoons cornstarch
4 tablespoons butter
juice of ½ lemon

Behind the Scenes — Soak raisins overnight in the brandy. Drain raisins from liquor. Mix sugar, salt, and cornstarch and turn into a pint measuring cup or bowl.

Before the Guests — Heat the water to boiling in the blazer pan. Stir slowly into the sugar and cornstarch; when smooth pour back into blazer pan and stir constantly until liquid is richly thick and *crystal* clear. (*Note* that so long as the sauce retains any whiteness of color the cornstarch is not yet completely cooked. *Crystal* clearness is the signal that cooking is complete; taste it to be sure cornstarch is cooked.) Add raisins, lemon juice and butter. Reheat. Stir in most of the brandy in which raisins were soaked. Pour remainder over top. Set ablaze. Serve over hot steamed pudding.

Tray-Maid

1) water
2) sugar and cornstarch mixed
3) raisins
4) butter
5) brandy
6) lemon juice

Holiday Airs

Apértif
Stuffed Roasted Bird
Stewed Cucumbers
Sweet Potato Glacé
Hot Fig Pudding with
Flaming Brandy Sauce

Bisque of Sea Food
2- Mushroom & Artichoke Hearts
63= Mushroom & Ham
69= Fondue Neuchâteloise
18 =136 Welsh Rarebit
29= Veal Paprika
80 = Beef Stroganoff
105= Chipped Beef in
Wine - Mushroom Sauce

139= Chicken Shortcake
157= Bananas Kroberg—
157= Heavenly Salmon Hash
183= Jigg's Favorite
226= Flaming Maple Sauce
227=   "   Fresh Apricot
228= Pear Flambée au Port
230= Royale Peaches Aflame
231= Brandied Bananas with Green grapes

Flaming Cherries Jubilee

no. 2 can black cherries
2 thin slices of lemon
¼ cup sugar
½ teaspoon cinnamon
½ cup brandy

Behind the Scenes — Pit the cherries.   Mix sugar and cinnamon.

Before the Guests — Heat (but do not boil) the cherries, with their juice and with the lemon slices, in the blazer pan of the chafing dish.   Sprinkle the prepared sugar over top, then add the brandy.   Set ablaze.   When flame dies down, blow (or fan) it out and serve at once over ice cream or squares of your favorite sponge cake.

Tray-Maid	*Happy Ending*
1) pitted cherries and cherry juice	Pistachio Ice Cream with Cherries Jubilee
2) sugar and cinnamon, mixed	Demi-tasse
3) lemon slices	Mints
4) brandy	Liqueur

Brandy Omelet with Almonds and Strawberries

1 pint strawberries
sugar for berries
2 eggs, separated
1 teaspoon lemon juice
dash of salt
2 tablespoons hot water

1 tablespoon granulated sugar
½ teaspoon salt
2 tablespoons sweet butter
powdered sugar
brandy
1 dozen blanched almonds

Behind the Scenes — This is a tricky dessert but practice makes perfect. Try it out before you perform before guests. Wash strawberries; do not hull. Sugar lightly just before serving. Separate eggs, place yolks and whites in separate mixing bowls. Note that sweet butter is used in blazer pan since it is less apt to stick.

Before the Guests — Beat egg whites with rotary beater until they stand in peaks. Then beat egg yolks (rotary beater will not have to be washed twice if whites are beaten first) until thick and lemon-colored. Continue to beat, adding sugar, salt, then the hot water and lemon juice. Fold in egg whites. Melt butter in blazer pan of chafing dish over flame. Pour in omelet. Let it cook for a few minutes undisturbed until crust begins to form, then begin to run a spatula around the edge to loosen omelet from pan. Continue with the spatula, working it further and further under the omelet until, by the time the omelet is brown on the bottom, it is quite free from the pan. Continue cooking until omelet appears to be cooked through. Sprinkle top liberally with powdered sugar, scatter the blanched almonds around sides of omelet. Pour brandy over top and set ablaze. You will find the brandy runs down into sides of pan, blazing there (as well as on top) to slightly toast the almonds. Fold over (as you would any omelet). Now sprinkle the brown side with a little powdered sugar. Pour additional brandy over top. Set ablaze. Serve at once, with the whole strawberries on the sides. Serves 4.

Tray-Maid

1) sweet butter
2) egg yolks
3) egg whites
4) berries
5) granulated sugar
6) brandy
7) powdered sugar
8) hot water
9) lemon juice
10) salt
11) almonds
12) rotary beater
13) spatula

Serving Suggestion: As a dessert this puffy 2-egg omelet will serve 4 generously. You will find it rich and satisfying. We would suggest that it follow a simple supper as a dramatic climax.

Pêches Flambées

      6 firm but fully ripe peaches
      1 cup water
      1 cup granulated sugar
        rum
        macaroon crumbs

Behind the Scenes — Plunge peaches in boiling water. Drain and peel. Halve and remove stones. Arrange small mounds of macaroon crumbs on six dessert plates. Set these aside on service table.

Before the Guests — Place the water and sugar in the lower pan of chafing dish. When sugar has dissolved poach peach halves in this syrup for 8 minutes. Transfer peaches to blazer pan and add just enough of the syrup to barely cover. Pour rum over peaches and set ablaze. Serve 2 halves on each mound of macaroon crumbs with sauce over top. Serves 6.

Tray-Maid	*Dinner Partners*
1) peaches pared, stoned and cut into halves	*Dress up a simple dinner with this exotic dessert service*
2) water	Grapefruit
3) sugar	Beanpot with Brown Bread
4) rum	Radishes Carrot Sticks
	Pêches Flambées
	Coffee with Cardamom Seed

Crêpes Suzette

12 French pancakes
½ cup butter
    grated rind of 1 orange
¼ cup powdered sugar
    juice of 2 oranges
½ cup Cointreau
½ cup brandy

Behind the Scenes — French pancakes may be purchased rolled and ready for reheating. Or you may prepare the pancakes by the recipe below. Grate the outside rind of the orange (not the inner white part, since this is bitter) and mix with the powdered sugar.

Before the Guests — Melt the butter in blazer pan of the chafing dish. When beginning to bubble with heat, add the crêpes and sprinkle prepared sugar over top. When crêpes are hot squeeze the orange juice into the pan; add the Cointreau; baste with this sauce until crêpes are deliciously flavorful. Pour brandy over top. Set it ablaze and as soon as flame dies down, serve the crêpes Suzette with some of the sauce over each. Serves 4.

Tray-Maid

1) crêpes
2) butter
3) sugar with orange rind
4) juice of orange
5) Cointreau
6) brandy

Crêpes Suzette

1 cup sifted flour
½ teaspoon salt
3 eggs well beaten
1 cup milk
Mix flour and salt, combine eggs and milk. Add flour and beat until smooth. Bake one at a time on a hot greased griddle, making cakes about 3" in diameter. Yield: about 12 crepes. Roll as a jelly roll or fold twice into neat squares.

Mulled Red Wine

2 cups simple syrup
4 sticks cinnamon
4 cloves
2 lemons, thinly sliced
1 pint (2 measuring cups) dry
    red wine

Behind the Scenes — Make a simple syrup by boiling together for 5 minutes 2 cups water with 1 cup sugar.

Before the Guests — Reheat the simple syrup in the blazer pan with the cinnamon and cloves. Add the slices of lemon; cover; remove from flame and let stand for 10 minutes. Return to flame; add wine. Reheat to piping hot. Place over hot water (in lower pan) and serve in punch glasses.

Tray-Maid	*Bridge Table Service*
1) simple syrup 2) cinnamon sticks and cloves 3) sliced lemon 4) wine	Mulled Red Wine, piping hot, is served in punch glasses. Tidbits such as cheese straws, cheese-stuffed celery, pickled mushrooms, toasted crackers with pot cheese, and mints are all popular accompaniments.

Café Brûlot

1 cup of brandy	4 sticks of cinnamon
8 lumps of sugar	10 whole cloves
the peel of an orange	3 cups of strong, fresh coffee

Behind the Scenes — Peel the orange into one long thin ribbon. Make the coffee by your favorite method. Heat the bowl of the chafing dish with hot water just before serving.

Before the Guests — Place the peel, cinnamon, cloves and 6 lumps of sugar in the bowl and pour in the brandy. Dip up some brandy in the ladle. Drop in the two remaining lumps of sugar and ignite. Ladle and pour back the flaming liquid scooping up the peel and sugar so that they too burn. Slowly and carefully add coffee and as the flame flickers out, ladle the café into demi-tasse cups. Serves 6 to 8.

Variation — For *Café Diablo* use even amounts of coffee and brandy, omit the cinnamon, and add the thinly sliced peel of lemon. Proceed as above.

Tray-Maid

1) brandy
2) sugar
3) orange peel
4) cinnamon
5) cloves
6) coffee
7) match
8) ladle

INDEX

INDEX

INDEX